WRITERS AND THEIR WORK

ISOBEL ARMSTRONG
General Editor

BRYAN LOUGHREY
Advisory Editor

ANGLO-SAXON VERSE

T0340595

Bede, from a twelfth-century manuscript of his *Life of St Cuthbert*.
By courtesy of the British Library, London.

ANGLO-SAXON VERSE

GRAHAM HOLDERNESS

Northcote House
in association with the
British Council

First published in 2000 by Northcote House Publishers Ltd, Horndon, Tavistock, Devon, PL19 9NQ, United Kingdom.
Tel: +44 (01822) 810066 Fax: +44 (01822) 810034.

British Library Cataloguing-in-Publication Data
A catalogue record for this book is available from the British Library

ISBN 0-7463-0914-7
Typeset by PDQ Typesetting, Newcastle-under-Lyme
Printed and bound in the United Kingdom

In memory of
Phyllis Rose Powrie
1915–1998

feran on frean

Contents

Acknowledgements

The following translations have been previously published:

Extract from 'The Husband's Message', *Christian Poetry Review*, 6 (April 1997), p. 8; 'The Ruin', *The Use of English*, 49:1 (Autumn 1997), pp. 62–3, and *Critical Survey* 10:2 (1998), pp. 61–2; 'The Dream of the Rood', *Literature and Theology*, 11:4 (Autumn 1997), pp. 366–71; 'The Seafarer' *Literature and Theology*, 11:4 (Autumn 1997), pp. 371–5; 'The Wanderer', *English*, 47: 188 (Summer 1998), pp. 99–102; 'Scyld's Funeral (from *Beowulf*)', *Critical Survey* 9:3 (1997), pp. 128–9; and *Iota Poetry Quarterly*, 44 (1998), p. 43; 'Wulf and Eadwacer', *The Use of English*, 50:2 (Spring 1999), pp. 155–6.

Material from chapter 4 published in *Literature and Theology*, 11:4 (Autumn 1997), pp. 347–65; material from Chapter 3 published in Liam Gearon (ed.), *English Literature, Theology and the Curriculum* (London: Cassell, 1999), pp. 63–84; material from the Introduction and Chapter 1 published in the *European English Messenger*, VIII:2 (Autumn 1999), pp. 34–7.

I should like to express my gratitude to Bryan Loughrey, John Burrow, and Graham Caie for extensive editorial suggestions, and to Carol Banks for assistance in developing the project.

Chronology of the Anglo-Saxon Period

1013	English submit to Sweyn, King of Denmark
1016–35	Cnut King of England
1042–66	Reign of Edward the Confessor
1066	Battle of Hastings

Introduction

Why read and study Anglo-Saxon poetry?

Although it is the primary linguistic basis of modern English, in 1066 the Anglo-Saxon language was culturally oppressed, along with England itself, by the French and Latin languages of the Norman conquerors. Thereafter the English language went through rapid and large-scale changes (see below, Chapter 1) that turned it into the later medieval language (such as that of Chaucer) which we can easily recognize as a form of English. By fairly soon after the eleventh century Anglo-Saxon had become a dead language, scarcely surviving in spoken use, its writing unintelligible until deciphered centuries later by scholars who had to reconstruct the language.

Anglo-Saxon is as much a foundational form of English as Latin is the root of Italian, French, and Spanish. Yet while Latin continued to be written and even spoken in England until the seventeenth century, Anglo-Saxon was dead by the early Middle Ages. Latin was preserved in consistent usage after the fall of Rome mainly because it was the language of the Christian church – for the English after the Conquest, the Latin 'Vulgate' Bible *was* the Christian scripture until English translations began to be made around the turn of the millennium. After 1066 Anglo-Saxon, the language of a conquered people, had no powerful institution to preserve or continue its usage, and so as a living language it soon ceased to exist.

Thus English culture has for a long time preserved a certain lop-sidedness in its approach to different aspects of its linguistic heritage. Since the English language was formed largely from both Germanic and Romance roots (on the one hand from 'Common Germanic', including Danish, on the other from Latin and French) educational traditions ought to have paid equal respects to both originating contexts. But Latin, though also a dead language, continued, and to some extent even now continues, to be an essential component of some educational programmes (it is still a compulsory element in the curriculum of more traditional independent schools, even for pupils of an early age). Anglo-Saxon, on the other hand, has never enjoyed a similar privilege.[1]

Early scholars of the Anglo-Saxon language were to some extent motivated by a kind of cultural nationalism, a desire to bring this hidden half of the English cultural heritage back into equal prominence with its Latin counterpart. At the beginning of this century scholars began to re-name Anglo-Saxon 'Old English': partly because the term 'Anglo-Saxon' is too narrow to reflect the full range of the early settlement of Britain and of formative linguistic influences on English (though this has never bothered historians, who are quite happy to continue talking about 'Anglo-Saxon England'); but mainly in order to locate Anglo-Saxon as an early form of English, preceding 'Middle' and 'Modern' English, rather than as some remote and barbaric foreign tongue. Hence in some ancient universities, as recently as the 1960s, Anglo-Saxon remained a compulsory component of the study of English Literature. When I attended the University of Oxford in the 1960s, my first term was occupied reading Latin, Anglo-Saxon, and the Latinate poetry of John Milton (or, as we used to describe the curriculum, 'three dead languages').[2]

Eventually, however, the educational question became not 'English or Latin?', but rather 'dead or living languages?'. By the time I had graduated and started teaching English at Oxford as a graduate assistant, its old induction course had been swept away and replaced by 'Literature 1900–1945'. Nowadays it is widely assumed that one learns other languages in order to be able to use them in the contemporary world, and hence the methods of language teaching themselves have completely changed, with much more emphasis on the learning by and for oral communication. In more conservative educational institutions there remains an attachment to the study of Latin as a linguistic foundation of English, and within the parameters of that argument, it would be difficult to justify the exclusion of Anglo-Saxon, which is the primary source of the English language.

But generally, interest in such ancient languages as Latin and Anglo-Saxon is cultural and historical rather than primarily linguistic. If we learn Latin we do so not in order to speak or write it, nor in order to improve the standard of our spoken and written English; but in order to gain access to the world of a founding historical civilization. We can understand the philosophy, religion, ethics, politics and law, and military strategy of ancient Rome in a uniquely inward way by reading Cicero and Caesar and Justinian in Latin. Above all, we need the language if we are to fully appreciate the literature, since literature can never be wholly reproduced in translation. And though it will sound like an exaggeration to say that years of learning Latin are justified by the pleasure and enlightenment one can acquire from reading Horace and Virgil, this is an affirmation that I (and probably many other lovers of literature) would none the less be prepared to make.

Exactly the same applies to Anglo-Saxon writing. A historical study of the Anglo-Saxon period provides an inexhaustibly interesting source of insights into the nature of a particular kind of society: a society which we can feel as in some ways similar to our own (for example, the ethnic diversity of Anglo-Saxon England compares to our own multicultural society, and the variety of religious beliefs that preceded and co-existed with Christianity parallels our own multifaith culture), but in many ways also very different from it. That sense of distance and difference is signalled very explicitly by the remoteness of the language.[3]

But for me the chief value of the Anglo-Saxon language is that it was used to create Anglo-Saxon literature, and specifically Anglo-Saxon poetry. The literature of the late Saxon period contains examples of poetic expression that are quite simply unequalled in any other language for beauty, for articulation of feeling, for philosophical profundity, and for depth of insight into human experience. What is probably one of the first Christian poems to be written in English, *The Dream of the Rood*, is still acknowledged as one of the greatest English Christian poems. In the heroic epic *Beowulf* readers have recognized the English equivalent of Homer's *Iliad* and Virgil's *Aeneid*. In elegiac poems like *The Wanderer* and *The Seafarer* we can find the expression of sentiments that belong wholly to their time and place, yet continue to reverberate with significance as unforgettable articulations of the fundamental nature of human existence. In the end, then, a struggle with Anglo-Saxon grammar and vocabulary is worth it for the access it gives to these permanently valuable poetic expressions.

But this study is written primarily for those who have little or no knowledge of the Old English language. For this reason the texts presented and discussed here are all my own translations, some written especially for this book, some previously published as independent poems (as mentioned in the Acknowledgements). I have provided in the conclusion some suggestions as to how a beginner might start to explore the poetry in its original tongue. But meanwhile, this book provides translations for the non-specialist reader that lie between the original poems and the modern English in which they now have to be discussed and interpreted.

I discuss the paradoxes of such translation in Chapter 1. Though full translations are provided here of all the texts discussed (some being extracts from longer poems), the critical discussions do refer to the original Anglo-Saxon poems in their own language, and some words and phrases are quoted in the text. Where this occurs, there is always a literal translation. Line numbers cited in the text always refer to the translations. To avoid confusion between the different line numbers in originals and translations, quotations from the original poems are identified by reference to a particular edition, and to that edition's line-numbering, always in endnotes. Apart from these references to primary material, the secondary works cited and recommended are generally of an accessible and introductory kind for the non-specialist student.

1

Anglo-Saxon Verse

CAEDMON'S 'HYMN'

In his *Ecclesiastical History* (completed in 731 AD) the Venerable Bede tells of Caedmon, a cowherd at the monastery of Streanaeshalch (Whitby), who

> had followed a secular occupation until well advanced in years without ever learning anything about poetry. Indeed it sometimes happened at a feast that all the guests in turn would be invited to sing and entertain the company; then, when he saw the harp coming his way, he would get up from the table and go home.
>
> On one such occasion he had left the house in which the entertainment was being held and went out to the stable where it was his duty that night to look after the beasts. There when the time came he settled down to sleep. Suddenly in a dream he saw a man standing beside him who called him by name. 'Caedmon,' he said, 'sing me a song.' 'I don't know how to sing,' he replied. 'It is because I cannot sing that I left the feast and came here.' The man who addressed him then said: 'But you shall sing to me.' 'What should I sing about?' he replied. 'Sing about the Creation of all things,' the other answered. And Caedmon immediately began to sing verses in praise of God the Creator that he had never heard before.[1]

The event is dated by Bede to 680 AD. Thereafter, the story continues, Caedmon found himself able to make wonderful poetry out of any scriptural source. His ability was immediately acknowledged by the leaders of the monastery as a gift from God:

> Early in the morning he went to his superior the reeve, and told him about this gift that he had received. The reeve took him before the abbess, who had ordered him to give an account of his dream and repeat the verses in the presence of many learned men, so that a decision might be reached by common consent as to their quality

1

and origin. All of them agreed that Caedmon's gift had been given to him by our Lord (p. 249).

Admitted as a brother to the monastery, Caedmon was 'instructed in the events of sacred history' (p. 249), and employed his poetic gift in a life of Christian service, making poems on all the great Old and New Testament narratives, from Genesis to Revelation. The divine gift was strictly conditional – he wasn't able, for instance, to compose anything but religious poetry: 'he could never compose any frivolous or profane verses; but only such as had a religious theme fell fittingly from his devout lips' (p. 249).

The story of Caedmon, as Bede tells it, provides a beautiful myth of origin for English Christian poetry.[2] A simple, unlettered man of humble occupation finds, through divine inspiration, a gift of eloquence (significantly, in a stable), which manifests itself naturally in his own vernacular language, English. Had he been educated and trained in the Church, he would of course have read and written in Latin, the language in which his scriptural sources were available to the literate. Those who gave him 'instruction' in Whitby Abbey took their learning from such texts as the Latin Vulgate, and communicated it orally, in English, to the lay population.[3] There was no English Bible before the end of the tenth century.[4]

Bede himself was writing his history in Latin, and although he describes in great detail the context in which Caedmon's poem was produced, he does not include the poem itself in his narrative. Instead he provides a Latin paraphrase –

> Nunc laudare debemus auctorem regni caelestis, potentiam Creatoris, et consilium illius, facta Patris gloriae; quomodo ille, cum sit aeternus Deus, omnium miraculorum auctor exstitit; qui primo filiis hominum caelum pro culmine tecti, dehinc terram custos humani generis omnipotens creavit.[5]

> ['Now we ought to praise the author of the heavenly kingdom, the power of the Creator, and His wisdom, the works of the Father of Glory; how He, as He is Eternal God, was maker of all wonders; who in the beginning provided for the sons of men the sky for a roof, then made the earth for humankind, the all-powerful protector'.]

He explains that poetry cannot be translated without irreparable damage: 'for verses, however masterly, cannot be translated literally from one language into another without losing much of their beauty and dignity' (p. 249). The Anglo-Saxon hymn itself appears in some manuscripts of the Latin history, either in the margin, at the foot of the page, or on another page. It didn't appear in its proper place in the narrative until Bede's work was translated into Old English.[6]

Caedmon's Hymn

Nu we sculan herian   *heofonrices Weard,*
Metodes mihte   *and his modgeþonc,*
weorc Wuldorfaeder;   *swa he wundra gehwaes,*
ece Dryhten,   *ord onstealde.*
He aerest gesceop   *eorðan bearnum*
heofon to hrofe,   *halig Scyppend;*
ða middangeard,   *moncynnes Weard,*
ece Dryhten,   *aefter teode*
firum foldan,   *Frea aelmightig.*

['Now we must praise   Heaven-kingdom's Guardian
the Lord's might   and His mind-thought
the work of the Father of Glory   for He each wonder
(Eternal God)   in the beginning established.
He first shaped   for earth's children
heaven for a roof   (Holy Maker)
then middle-earth   (Mankind's Protector,
(Eternal God)   He afterwards created
the earth for men   (Lord Almighty)'].

It is assumed that the poem we have is an authentic version from which Bede made his paraphrase. But frankly, for all we know, since the manuscript records of the Old English poem are later than Bede's narrative, the Old English versions may have been made from Bede's Latin, and Caedmon's poem itself may have been an 'original' lost in the wonder of his dream. None of the other poems mentioned have survived, though there are several long poems on Biblical themes (see Chapter 4) which have naturally been associated with Caedmon.[7]

Thus by making a vernacular English poem in response to a clear divine prompting, Caedmon produced the first hymn of the English church, and single-handedly founded the beginnings of a vernacular English liturgy in the midst of a thoroughly Latinate ecclesiastical culture. It is entirely fitting, therefore, that he should have sung of the Creation, since he was evidently deploying the power of that same Almighty Creator to fashion something completely new and unprecedented. In this miracle, God was simultaneously manifesting His power to unstop the tongue of the dumb; making a learned poet out of an illiterate and uneducated cowherd; and, through Caedmon, both founding a new literary language, and shaping a new form of poetic expression.

OLD ENGLISH: LANGUAGE AND LITERATURE

At this point, however, it is necessary to question some of the tenets of Bede's compelling myth. God may have made the universe out of nothing, but Caedmon certainly did not invent either the language in which he sang, or the verse-form he employed as a basis for his hymn. On the contrary, the origins of the alliterative verse-form he used, and one which remains the standard verse-form for all the surviving examples of Old English verse written between the seventh and the eleventh centuries, go far back beyond the conversion of the English to Mediterranean Christianity (dated from 597 AD, when St Augustine arrived in Britain) into a northern and pagan Germanic past.

The English language arrived on these islands with the immigration of Germanic peoples – Jutes, Saxons, Angles – from the European mainland at the time of Roman withdrawal from Britain, or even earlier, with the Germanic tribesmen serving in the Roman army. Old English is one of the Germanic languages which linguists believe derived from a prehistoric Common Germanic (one of the putative 'Indo-European' languages) spoken in southern Scandinavia and northern Germany. From this common Germanic, it is argued, there developed several different individual languages: East Germanic (which survives in written evidence as Gothic); North Germanic, the basis of the Scandinavian languages; and West Germanic, from which derived Old High German, Old Saxon, Old Frisian, and Old English. A coin dating from 450–500 AD displays in a runic inscription traces of both Old English and Old Frisian languages.[8] By the fifth century AD, some form of Germanic speech was common along the east coast of England, having

4

replaced both British (now Welsh) and the colloquial Latin of the Romans. British place-names recorded in legal charters disappear in favour of Old English ones: thus a charter dated to about 692 AD, granting lands to Barking Abbey, includes Old English place-names within the Latin text.[9]

Different versions of the Germanic language took root in different parts of the country, eventually forming variant dialects of the common Old English language. The separate kingdoms of Northumbria, Mercia, Kent, and Wessex each had its own different dialect. Caedmon's hymn is again a useful illustration of this point. The oldest examples of the hymn (c.735) are in the dialect of the Northumbrian Kingdom, which stretched south as far as the Humber (and at certain periods beyond it), and which contained Whitby.[10] Later versions of the hymn, like the one reproduced above, were written some time after that, in West Saxon. Most of the written records of Anglo-Saxon England are in West Saxon, as a consequence of the later political and cultural dominance of Wessex, boosted by King Alfred's concern to develop literacy, and reaching its peak when Aethelstane became 'king of all England' in the tenth century. 'Old English' continued to be written until about 1150, though the social basis which maintained it as an almost purely Germanic language disappeared, of course, with the Norman Conquest in 1066.

Though the Anglo-Saxon language underwent during its currency some substantial historical shifts (for example, grammatical and lexical changes under the influence of Scandinavian invaders), it was the period from 1100 to 1500 which saw the major structural changes that started to make 'Old English' seem something of a foreign tongue to us. An inflected language (one in which words change their shape in response to their grammatical function, as in French and German) changed to one with hardly any inflexional endings; sound changes affected the pronunciation and spelling of the vocabulary; many native words were lost and replaced by borrowings from other languages, particularly French and Latin. Hence the Middle English used in the southeast of England, which appears in the work of fourteenth-century writers like Chaucer, is far more accessible to a modern English reader than its Anglo-Saxon predecessor.[11]

5

But the verse form used by Caedmon had its roots in that same Germanic and pagan past from which the language itself was derived. The alliterative verse line, consisting of short verse-phrases linked by stress and alliteration rather than by rhyme or metre, was a verse form commonly used for vernacular poetry throughout all the Germanic peoples, and was brought to Britain by the migrating tribes of the fifth century. It is rooted in an oral tradition of poems composed, performed, and transmitted without ever reaching a written form. Such a context of oral performance is clearly depicted by Bede in the Caedmon story, where the harp is shown going round at the feast, and members and guests of the community are asked in turn to offer a song. It is assumed that these people, like Caedmon, were illiterate, and that therefore their songs were learned or improvised from the resources of an oral tradition.

ORAL POETRY

Oral poets compose by taking well-known stories or other narratives (notably, in this period, the heroic tales of the Germanic past, and the grand narratives of the Bible) and giving them new expression within a regulated verse form. The verse form was evidently performed as a kind of rhythmical chanting to percussive or musical accompaniment, and therefore had to be free enough to allow for improvisation within a continuous movement. On the other hand, the phrases used by the poets were to a large extent stock formulae drawn from an established and familiar reservoir of such phrases; the Old English coinage *word-hord* ('word-stock') exactly describes such a body of linguistic materials:

> Whereas a lettered poet of any time and place, composing (as he does and must) with the aid of writing materials and with deliberation, creates his own language as he proceeds, the unlettered singer, ordinarily composing rapidly and extempore before a live audience, must and does call upon a ready-made language, upon a vast reservoir of formulas filling just measures of verse. These formulas develop over a long period of time; they are the creation of countless generations of singers and can express all the ideas a singer will need in order to tell his story, itself usually traditional.[12]

6

Within the narrative of *Beowulf*, a poet is described composing in exactly this way:

> One of Hrothgar's thanes blithely began
> To skilfully recount Beowulf's bravery.
> He was a man endowed with words,
> His memory mindful of many an old
> Song, stored with a stock
> Of ancient stories. To tell an old tale
> New words he would weave, appropriate
> And pleasing, artistically linked,
> Suiting the subject, verbally varied
> Cleverly composed, and sweetly sung.[13]

The poet goes on to draw a parallel between Beowulf's killing of Grendel, and the mythical deeds of Sigmund the dragon-slayer from Germanic mythology.

Scholars have shown that Old English poetry can be analysed in such a way as to identify these formulae: F. P. Magoun, in the essay quoted above (pp. 194–201), showed that the first twenty-five lines of Beowulf contain no phrase that isn't shared, either somewhere else in the same poem, or in another. The point is particularly striking in view of the fact that only about 30,000 lines of Old English poetry survive from what must have been a much larger corpus, and that *Beowulf* itself, at over 3000 lines, represents over 10 per cent of the whole. Certainly if you look again at Caedmon's *Hymn*, you can see that within its nine lines there are no less than seven phrases, never quite the same, but all standing for one thing: God. Ironically, in creating the new form of Old English Christian poetry, Caedmon is shown using an 'oral-formulaic' medium which can only work if there is already a pre-existing stock of well-used and familiar literary phrases!

There can be little doubt that the surviving body of Old English poetry harks back to its origins in a Germanic oral tradition. But here, of course, we hit yet another fundamental paradox. If such poetry had continued to function in an oral tradition, then we could have had no record of it at all. We would have to imagine an England that had remained untouched by the literacy that came with Mediterranean Christianity; a culture in which the language remained a vernacular, spoken language, short extracts of which would have been scratched in runic script on coins, stones, and bits of wood;[14] and a culture whose poetry would have remained a purely oral form until it became captured, say, as the ballads of Scotland were captured by eighteenth-century antiquarians from another land.

The fact is, of course, that in the seventh century the Christian missionaries from Rome and Gaul brought with them literacy, reading and writing, and the English very quickly became a lettered people.[15] As a consequence of that incursion the poetic records are written down in manuscripts. Caedmon's poem, supposedly composed in 680 AD, actually dates from manuscripts of the eighth century. Almost all the other surviving Old English poetry exists in manuscripts written in the tenth and eleventh centuries. We know that some of the poetry is certainly much older than the written record (for example lines from *The Dream of the Rood*, recorded in a manuscript of the later tenth century, are found on a stone cross that possibly dates from as early as 670 AD). But although there is much scholarly argument about the dates of composition for these poems, scholars cannot with any certainty finally date any of the poems with anything like the accuracy with which they can date the manuscripts. Though *The Dream of the Rood* may go back as far as the seventh century, its companion-piece in the same manuscript, Cynewulf's *Elene*, can only have been a literary work, since, like Cynewulf's other poems, it contains the poet's signature encoded in a runic acrostic, a puzzle that only works in writing.[16]

A number of scenarios for the composition and transmission of these poems is possible. Some of the heroic poems, such as *Beowulf*, could be very old indeed (fifth- or sixth-century), having existed within the oral tradition for centuries before they came to England. They could have continued to develop here within an oral repertoire – oral poems, of course, never have a fixed text, but continue to change over time – and could have been captured almost as 'antiquities' by lettered people of the tenth and eleventh centuries.

On the other hand, those writers of the tenth and eleventh centuries could have composed these poems from their knowledge of traditional poetic materials, in the way that, for instance, in the early Middle Ages, Icelandic sagas were written down from old traditional oral sources.[17] In this case *Beowulf*, though its narrative materials and general artistic form may have been very old, would never have existed as a whole poem in the form that it has reached us, before a date that scholars now think may have been as late as somewhere between 850 and 1000. *The Battle of Maldon*, which has so much in common with traditional heroic poetry, tells of a historical event that took place in 991.

In *Beowulf* itself we find another description of poetry being performed, this time at a feast, exactly as in the story of Caedmon. Here the performance is rendered by a *scop*, a court poet who possesses professional skills (*saegde se þe cuþe*, 'he sang who knew how'),[18] rather than by amateurs on the 'have-a-go' system described by Bede. But the poet sings, in the same social context of a communal feast and entertainment, to the accompaniment of a harp; and he sings, coincidentally, of the Creation. The monster Grendel overhears the song:

> A ferocious fiend, dwelling in darkness,
> Dreadful days of denial endured
> When he heard from the hall the ring of
> Rejoicing, the harp's clear harmony, the poet's
> Sweet song. For that minstrel sang,
> With a sonorous skill, of the ancient origins
> Of humankind: of how the Almighty
> Fashioned the firmament, a shining surface,
> Surrounded by sea. He hung in the heavens
> The sun and the moon, to provide all people
> With seasons and signs; and on the deep's darkness,
> He let there be light. He clothed earth's contours
> With flora and foliage, and the breath in their bodies
> He gave to the beasts. All that has life
> The earth brought forth.

> (*Beowulf*, Part I, 101–15)

If *Beowulf* did ever exist as an oral poem or poems, then it would have been performed in just such a context. If it included this passage, it would have functioned (like a 'play-within-a-play'), as a song-within-a-song, and the singer would have been dramatizing himself and his own performative role. Strangely enough, however, in this heroic poem of *geardagum* ('yesteryear'[19]) – itself assumed to be the product of an oral tradition, and in the very passage where oral poetry is described in its context – the actual 'Song of Creation' is far more *literary* than is Caedmon's hymn on

9

the same subject.[20] One can imagine an amateur singer, who had been taught the story of Creation from the Bible, putting together an account which combines selected elements of the Biblical narrative with formulaic celebrations of God's creative attributes: and it would look something like Caedmon's hymn. But the *scop* in *Beowulf* offers a detailed versification of Genesis,[21] listing the sequential stages of Creation – the earth and the waters, the sun and moon, vegetation and the beasts of the field. The poem-within-a-poem, though orally delivered, follows the narrative sequence of the Old Testament in a detailed versification of a written source. Where Caedmon's poem displays the repetitive, cyclical, and formulaic features of oral composition, the Creation poem in *Beowulf* is remarkably free of repetition or any other oral characteristic.

MANUSCRIPT SOURCES

The only certainties informing our approach to Old English poetry lie in the facts of their material provenance, that is, the form in which they were recorded and transmitted to posterity. On this basis we can confidently generalize that all Old English poetry, however and whenever composed, was committed to record in the environment of a literate and Christian culture. Although there are clearly connections in the poetry with a pre-Christian and oral culture of the past, they remain irreversibly coloured by the conditions within which the poems were written down. Exactly how historic and contemporary influences interacted is discussed at the level of the individual poem in the chapters that follow. In general we could say that scholarly and critical approaches which focus more closely on material written records than on speculations about, for instance, oral composition and transmission, are more likely to see these poems as 'modern' in their own time than as carefully preserved antiques. Early critics, for instance, used to see *Beowulf* as a thoroughly pagan poem, to which a Christian colouring had been added in the course of monastic preservation.[22] Later scholars have been more likely to see the poem as a wholly Christian work, with its uses of older materials thoroughly subordinated to a modern world-view.[23] It is tempting to view an elegy like *The Wanderer* as a poem largely of pagan sentiment, with a few formal Christian elements, including a preface and conclusion, added to give it a superficial doctrinal respectability. But *The Wanderer* sits in the *Exeter Book* next to the completely and indisputably Christian *Seafarer*, and the interaction of apparently 'pagan' and formally Christian elements in both poems seems to me a more complicated matter than simple scribal tampering, or ecclesiastical appropriation.[24]

All the poems contained within this study, apart from Caedmon's *Hymn* and *The Battle of Maldon*, are to be found in one of four major collections of Old English verse and prose, all of which date from the second half of the tenth century: the *Beowulf* Manuscript (British Museum Cotton Vitellius A.xv); the 'Exeter Book', in the library of Exeter Cathedral; the 'Vercelli Book' (*Codex Vercellensis*), in the chapter library of the cathedral at Vercelli in northern Italy; and the 'Junius Manuscript' (Junius 11, Bodleian Library, Oxford). The manuscript of *The Battle of Maldon* was destroyed in 1731 by a fire (which also damaged the *Beowulf* manuscript), and has survived through an eighteenth-century edition and an earlier transcript.

The *Beowulf* manuscript bears the signature of Lawrence Nowell, a sixteenth-century pioneer of Old English studies, together with the date 1563; so it was known of in Shakespeare's time. By 1705 it was in the library of Sir Robert Cotton. The poem was lucky to survive the Cottonian fire of 1731, and the manuscript was extensively damaged. An Icelandic scholar living in Copenhagen, Thorkelin, had the manuscript copied near the end of the eighteenth century, and an edition of the poem was eventually produced with the help of this copy in 1815. The burnt manuscript itself was rebound in the middle of the nineteenth century, the rebinding process covering from sight many letters on the edges of the pages. Recently the British Library has facilitated the copying of the manuscript into computerized digital images which, it is claimed, provide better visual access to its contents than could be achieved by the naked eye (for example, letters hidden under tape in rebinding can be back-lighted and captured in the digital image).[25]

The 'Exeter Book' was given by Leofric, Bishop of Devon and Cornwall and Edward the Confessor's Chancellor, to Exeter Cathedral. It consists entirely of poetry, and contains (of the poems translated here) *The Ruin, The Wanderer, The Seafarer, The Wife's Lament* and *Wulf and Eadwacer*. The 'Vercelli Book' has probably been in the cathedral library at Vercelli for six or seven centuries. It contains, among other Christian poems, *The Dream of the Rood*. The 'Junius Manuscript' is named after the Huguenot scholar Junius, who printed its poems in 1655 as the works of Caedmon, since the manuscript contains poems answering very exactly to Bede's description of Caedmon's poetic output – *Genesis, Exodus, Daniel, Christ and Satan. The Fall of the Angels*, discussed below in Chapter 4, appears in the Junius manuscript as part of a poem on the stories of *Genesis* (*Genesis B*).

Taking the whole surviving corpus of Old English verse (as indicated above, some 30,000 lines) as a totality, we find within it certain clearly distinct categories of poetry, for each of which there are some or many examples. There are the heroic poems, among which *Beowulf* stands out as the biggest complete Old English poem. Heroic poetry can be legendary (like *Widsith*, an epic of heroic adventures in a legendary Europe, or the fragmentary *Waldere*, which deals with the same Germanic legends as does Wagner's *Ring*[26]); or historical, like *The Battle of Maldon*. Then there is the form of the 'elegy', poems like *The Ruin, The Wanderer,* and *The Seafarer*, which lament a lost past, often in the form of a dramatic monologue. The two latter poems are explicitly Christian, and merge traditional pagan nostalgia with Christian meditations on the transience and fragility of all human life. Other types of Christian poetry are those based on scriptural or patristic sources, like *Genesis, Exodus, Daniel, Christ and Satan*; verse lives of saints, such as *Juliana, Guthlac, Elene*; and poems of a devotional, meditative, and theological kind, like *Judgement Day I and II* and *The Dream of the Rood*. There survives a small handful of poems, lyrical and dramatic, that can be loosely termed 'love poems': *The Wife's Lament, The Husband's Message, Wulf and Eadwacer*.[27]

This study is inevitably selective, and it should be mentioned that there are many other Old English poems of the same and different types. There are poetic 'Charms', to be used against warts, dwarves, or cattle-thieves. There are many ingenious and well-crafted 'Riddles', little puzzles in verse. There is a group of 'bestiary' poems, exploiting the religious symbolism of animals like the whale and the phoenix. There are Christian liturgical

12

poems, such the *Lord's Prayer I, II* and *III*, and the *Gloria I* and *II*. Lastly there are the so-called 'Gnomic' verses, collections of wise and witty sayings and philosophical observations.[28] Taken together, these diverse poetic records indicate something of the varieties of Anglo-Saxon verse; and of the many uses, practical as well as artistic, to which poetry was once put.

TRANSLATION

This study is written for those who are unable to read Old English poetry, in its original language, in the way that poetry needs to be read. So the texts cited and discussed are not the Old English poems themselves, but my own modern trans-lations of them.

In one sense, translation is impossible. There is no substitute for reading a literary artefact, particularly a poem, in its original language. But at the same time, communication is indispensable. Just as translation is essential for reciprocal understanding between peoples, so cultures can only speak, or listen to one another, through translation.

No-one can speak Anglo-Saxon. It is a dead language, and for those who speak its modern legacy, English, it appears to be a foreign tongue, which seems to bear more resemblance to contemporary German than to modern English. But even a scholar who has learned every extant word and grammatical element of Anglo-Saxon cannot know either the language, or its literature, in the way that a modern language and literature can be learned and known.

As indicated above, the term 'Old English' was substituted earlier this century, by scholars of language and literature, for 'Anglo-Saxon', partly to domesticate and familiarize the language, to suggest that it was only a stage in the development of English, only a step or two back from the perfectly legible and accessible language of Chaucer. In the new European Union it is now time to recognize Anglo-Saxon as precisely an inter-national, multicultural historical language: not one of the solid foundations of a homogenous English national culture, but rather an indicator of the varied cultural roots from which our polyglot mongrel tongue was originally formed.

13

Access to the learning of Anglo-Saxon is an increasingly restricted privilege. I learned it at Oxford at a time when it remained a compulsory 'gatekeeper' for undergraduate study in English. For the vast majority even of Literature students today, the Anglo-Saxon language remains a closed book. Hence the need for translation, by those perhaps accidentally gifted with that privilege, if these poems are to be widely enjoyed and appreciated.

But what kind of translation? Verse translation can have a number of purposes, but every example must entail at least two: to convey to the modern reader some of the poetic and imaginative qualities locked away in that inaccessible tongue; and to achieve some conformity between the original poetry and the idioms of traditional and contemporary English verse. The verse translation must sound, in its rhythm and phrasing, the echo of an antique drum; but in such a way as to make music to the modern ear.

Verse translations of Anglo-Saxon poetry range from what might be called the 'imitative', designed to reproduce in modern English the rhythmic and phonetic character of the original; and the 'assimilation', which aims to achieve some conformity between the original poetry and the traditional norms of English verse form. The strength of the imitative mode lies in its power to evoke the muscularity and concreteness of the old verse form; its weakness in a propensity to archaism and obscurity. The assimilationist mode familiarizes cultural strangeness and renders it acceptable to the contemporary sensibility; its corresponding disadvantage is a tendency to surrender to current poetic convention.

We can see examples of these types in different translations of a line from *The Dream of the Rood*. The original reads:

> *Feala ic on þam beorge   gebiden haebbe*
> *Wraðra wyrda*[29]
>
> (Many I on that hill   endured have
> dreadful fates)

An example of 'assimilative' rendering is Richard Hamer's (from *A Choice of Anglo-Saxon Verse*):

> And I underwent
> Full many a dire experience on that hill.[30]

14

Both the neo-medieval, Tennysonian archaism of 'full many' and the polysyllabic abstraction of 'experience' for *wyrda* (literally 'fates' or 'destinies') are instrumental in producing the metrical regularity and smooth flow of the conventional iambic pentameter. The voice is that of some lost knight of Victorian chivalry, rather than the tormented utterance of an anthropomorphized cross.

An extreme contrast can be found in Michael Alexander's 'imitative' translation (from *The Earliest English Poems*):

> Wry wierds a many I underwent
> up on that hill-top[31]

Alexander successfully imitates the original in rhythm and consonantal assonance, producing a compelling and strongly accented poetic emotion. But by punctiliously mimicking the Anglo-Saxon words *wraðra wyrda* he produces a phrase ('wry wierds') which is merely odd and idiosyncratic rather than effective as modern English translation. The concentrated syntax that created the powerful concreteness of Anglo-Saxon poetry disappeared when our Germanic language lost most of its inflectional endings, and introduced in their place auxiliary verbs and prepositions. Hence attempts like Michael Alexander's to revert to Anglo-Saxon syntax may succeed in echoing the original in form, but fail as translations; while fully assimilationist translations lose contact with the rhythmic and phonetic character of the original, sacrificing ancient form to the convenience of an accessible poetic vernacular.

My approach to translation operates self-consciously along the spectrum flanked at either end by imitation and assimilation. The versions are, for example, syntactically much looser and more expansive than the originals, precisely in order to avoid the obscurity of archaism (though with those poems whose verse-phrasing is particularly condensed, like *Beowulf*, I've sought a similar brevity and tightness of phrasing). The characteristic concreteness and muscular energy of the poetic language is then replaced by the use of more alliteration than the Old English originals (I frequently place at least two alliterative consonants in each half-line). The central line-break is elided, partly to avoid the mechanistic effect of repeated syntactical units, and generally to free the verse to attempt long,

15

energetic prosodic movements (the familiar lineation is in any case a modern editorial convention: in the original manuscripts the verse was simply written continuously from one side of the page to the other, with spaces or points between half-lines).

In terms of metre a continuous effort to eschew the reassuring regularity of iambic pentameter is persistently haunted by its stubborn reassertion. But heavily accented syllabic lines of free verse with strong alliteration and assonance are as familiar in modern verse as the iambic pentameter was to the Victorians. Everywhere in English poetry, into the fourteenth century in the poems of Langland and the *Gawain*-poet, and then from the later nineteenth century onwards in the 'sprung rhythm' of Gerard Manley Hopkins, the trochaic and dactylic music of Dylan Thomas, the tough 'masculinity' of Ted Hughes's verse, we can find traces of that consonantal repetition that seems a natural feature of the English language, and can even be imagined, if fancifully, as echoing indirectly down from the meadhalls of Anglo-Saxon England.[32]

Lastly, I have taken very wide liberties with metaphor and phrasing, and have not been averse to adding elements to the poems (for example, a more overtly Christian language, derived from translations of the scriptures made hundreds of years after the Anglo-Saxon poems themselves) which would certainly be challenged by purist translators; but which seem to me justified, in terms of reproducing, for the modern reader, a 'multicultural' poetry. In translating, as in interpreting the writing of the past, there is no way in which we can unlearn our own culture.

In personal terms the translator inevitably becomes a poor substitute for the absent and usually anonymous author, transmitting the Chinese whispers of a message repeated and re-interpreted many times before. In one sense translation is a natural extension of critical interpretation, an elaborate rereading that becomes an attempt at rewriting. To some extent the translator is the perfect postmodern critic, the reader as author, extrapolating the detail of a literary appreciation into a parallel, derivative, but quasi-creative construction. But just as in critical rewriting there can come a point where the critic disengages from the work under consideration and enters a domain of self-preoccupation (and this, of course, is the point where resistance to theoretical criticism is most likely to arise), so the translator is in continual danger of finding himself enthusiastically explicating a text that has quietly dropped back into the oubliette of time. This observation returns me to my earlier defence of Anglo-Saxon studies: just as in order to identify the point where a critic shifts from reading to theoretical disquisition the reader would have to know the work in question, so in order to assess whether my translations are genuine scholarly 'versions' or the self-indulgences of a poet manqué, the reader would need some direct acquaintance with the Anglo-Saxon language. As a gesture of encouragement towards that desirable aim, I have supplied as an appendix an example of original Anglo-Saxon verse with the modern translation explicated and explained (see pp. 94–7).

The translation of ancient works should entail an engagement with the past, demanding an openness to the archaic and obscure, as well as the will to open up in contemporary language a new space capable of admitting the remembered but unfamiliar guest. By all means let us continue to apprehend the Anglo-Saxon world as strange; but let us also follow Hamlet's injunction and 'as a stranger give it welcome'.

2

Heroic Poetry

BEOWULF (PART I)

Hey! We've heard of the glory
Of the good old days, how the worthy
Warriors of the warlike Danes
Wonders accomplished. You've heard
How Scyld Scefing, a destitute   5
Foundling, struck fear into enemies,
Ravaged and raided, plundered for
Prize. You must also have heard
How he thrived on that traffic,
Accumulating honour, waxing in wealth,   10
Till every last one of his neighbouring kings
To his power submitted, his tribute
Paid. Surely Scyld Scefing
Was the rarest of rulers! Later to him
A boy was born, a successor for Scyld,   15
A gift from God to console his kin
For the suffering they'd felt in their leaderless
Days. In exchange for those evils,
The God of Glory, the Lord of all life,
Granted abundance of honour to his heir: 20
So Beow, Scyld's son, became rich in renown
Among all those who dwelt
In the land of the Danes. Although still under
Paternal protection, a young man should always
Ensure by his actions, by the fair generosity   25
Of his freedom with gifts, that later he'll earn
The love and the loyalty of chosen
Companions, who'll hasten to help him
In the storm of strife. So everywhere men,
In all lands and all peoples, succeed and prosper   30
By praiseworthy deeds.

At the destined day, Scyld took ship,
Shaped his course, certain and sure,
And set his sail for the Lord's kingdom.
Faithful friends carried his corpse   35
To the ocean's edge, as he had asked them,
That loved and long-reigning lord of lands,
The shield of the Scyldings, while he himself
Could still wield words. Icy and eager,
The beaked boat bobbed on the white wave: 40
A hero's haulage heaved in the harbour.
There they laid down their cherished chief,
That generous giver, in the boat's bosom,
Mighty, though fallen, at the mast's foot.
Fortune afforded troves of treasure,   45
Travelled from afar, to embellish that bark:
I never heard of a vessel invested
With so many valuables, blades and byrnies
And weapons of war. The brightest and best
Of this warrior's wealth lay on his breast,   50
To pay for his passage on that vast voyage.
He went as he came, as abundantly endowed
In his faring forth as his hoving hither,
When those who consigned him – an infant alone,
But blessed with the best of the people's wealth –   55
Launched the lad on the way of the waves.
Gleaming with gold, high overhead
They set up his standard, and heavy of heart,
Mournful in mind, they let the tide take him,
Committed his corpse again to the deep.   60
But no-one can tell in absolute truth –
Neither the crafty counsellor in court,
Nor the brave soldier beneath the blue sky –
– Who, at the last, unloaded that cargo.

So, in those old days, Beow the Scylding   65
Was famed among folk as a popular king,
After his father, that excellent elder,
Dying in dignity, departed this earth.
Beow in time took his turn to be father:
His son was Halfdane, the haughty hero,   70
Who survived as sovereign, for the Scyldings'
Delight, to a war-hardened, ripe old age.
High Halfdane himself then sired four offspring:
Heorogar, and Hrothgar, and Halga the Good;

And Yrse, a girl, but a warrior's wife –   75
It was she who they chose as Onela's queen,
So she slept in a battle-hard Scylding's bed.
It was Hrothgar's fate to win fortune in
Fight, so his fame won him loyalty
From keen companions, with courageous retainers   80
His retinue grew. An ambition awoke
In Hrothgar's heart, to command the construction
Of a mighty mead-hall, the biggest building
In all human history, there to distribute,
To infant and elder, the gifts he'd received –   85
All the wealth of the world, save
Lands and life – by the grace of God.
The news became known, throughout all the
Tribes, that a work was wanted,
A construction commissioned. The next they knew,   90
It was fitted and furnished, finished, that finest
And hugest of halls. 'Heorot' Hrothgar
Nobly named it, princely potentate,
Lord of lands. Proud in his pleasure,
With rings he rewarded his folk at the feast.   95
High and horn-turreted towered the hall –
Though a darker destiny was biding its time,
Of savage slaughter, and flickering flame.
A future foreboded, where vicious feud
Would rudely awaken war's sleeping sword.   100

A ferocious fiend, dwelling in darkness,
Dreadful days of denial endured
When he heard from the hall the ring of
Rejoicing, the harp's clear harmony, the poet's
Sweet song. For that minstrel sang,   105
With a sonorous skill, of the ancient origins
Of humankind: of how the Almighty
Fashioned the firmament, a shining surface,
Surrounded by sea. He hung in the heavens
The sun and the moon, to provide all people   110
With seasons and signs; and on the deep's darkness,
He let there be light. He clothed earth's contours
With flora and foliage, and the breath in their bodies
He gave to the beasts. All that has life
The earth brought forth. So Hrothgar's heroes   115
Dwelt in delight, till a wanderer from Hell
Came to work them harm. This fearful phantom

Was known as Grendel. In the fens was his
Fastness: monarch of marshes, he moved
On the moors. For a time he held sway,   120
This sorrowful spirit, over that cursed kingdom,
The devils' domain; but later the Lord
His presence proscribed, condemned him together
With all Cain's kin, when the killing of Abel
By a curse he avenged. He took no delight,   125
The Lord, in Cain's deed: but drove him that day
From the face of the earth, banished the cruel
Killer of kin from human company,
Cain for his crime. All evil creatures
Claim kinship from Cain: ogres, and elves,   130
Monsters of might, and the giants who offered
Violence to God, till in the deep deluge
They reaped their reward.

PARTS XI–XII
(BEOWULF'S FIGHT WITH GRENDEL)
(ll. 710–836)

From the high moors, through the white hill-fog,
Grendel came gliding: carrying God's curse;
Meaning to murder a share of the sleepers
In that high hall. Beneath the clouds' shelter,
He silently stole, till he sighted, through shadows,   5
Of gold-gleaming Heorot the glittering roof.
He'd been there before, though none had invited him,
To Hrothgar's home. But never before, and never again
Did he get such a greeting from such a hard host!
On his joyless journey the creature came creeping   10
And arrived at the hall. The iron-bound barrier
Burst from its hinges at a blow from his hand;
In his rage he wrenched the door from its frame.
In a moment the monster had stepped on the pavement:
The flames of hell-fire flared from his eyes.   15
There in the hall, soundly asleep,
Lay a huddle of heroes, a brotherly band.
He inwardly exulted with a monstrous mirth
Determined, before daybreak enlightened the east,
Since fortune afforded him, famished, such fare,   20
To breakfast on blood, and bite into bones.

21

He could hardly know then, that fate had determined
To cease the supply of men for his meals.
For keeping a close watch, Hygelac's kinsman
Patiently perused his plan of attack.   25
Grendel intended no delay in his dining,
But greedily grabbed a soldier from his slumber:
Gorging on gristle and biting through bone
He slashed through his skin, invaded his veins,
And the liquid life-force drank at a draught.   30
Swiftly and soon he'd devoured the dead,
From feet to fingers, from top to toe.
Ready, resolved, the brave-hearted hero
Rose from his rest, and grappled Grendel
In a grievous grip; clearly conceiving   35
His evil intentions, grimly he grabbed
At an outstretched arm. Grendel soon gathered
That he'd never known, in all his wide wanderings
Throughout this world, a man with so mighty
Power in his palm. He'd never endured,   40
That monarch of mischief, the hold of so hard a hand.
At the core of his courage there grew a great fear:
Though he trembled in terror, he'd no hope of escape,
No freedom to fly. To disappear in the darkness
Was his strongest desire, to slyly slink back   45
To his devil's domain. Not through life's length
Had he ever encountered, unwilling,
Such a welcome. Then that bold Beowulf,
Bravely remembering his previous promise,
Leapt to his feet, and grappled with Grendel.   50
Knuckles cracked. Grendel put up
A desperate struggle, as the attacker closed in.
The demon desired to flee far away,
To hide in his home on the far-flung fens,
When his fingers he felt in the foeman's grip.   55
His trip to Heorot he truly regretted!

The rafters resounded to the sound of that struggle;
Astonished by terror stood the trembling Danes.
Two furious foes fought the place to possess;
With the din of the duel the edifice filled.   60
Who would believe that that noble building
Would withstand the stress of so cruel a combat?
You'd have guessed it would give, collapse on its
Columns, fissure, fragment, its foundations

Fall. That just goes to show how cleverly   65
Constructed, how skilfully wrought
Was the base of that building,
Skilfully sutured both inside and out,
Bolstered with brackets of unbreakable iron.
That's not to say that they did no damage,   70
Those ferocious fighters; for many a mead-bench,
Gilded with gold, did they snatch from the floor
And fracture to fragments. Before this combat,
Even the smartest men of the Scyldings
Had never considered such havoc could happen,   75
Such disaster occur. They thought that nothing, no human
Hand, could break and batter to rack and to ruin
That big and brilliant, bone-adorned building,
Unless flaring fire enveloped it in flames.

Then a new and insistent noise arose   80
And a shiver of terror tore each Dane's heart,
When they heard, one and all, the ear-splitting yelp
Of a fearsome demon in fear of his death.
A wounded wailing echoed from the walls,
The crippled keening of God's great adversary   85
Howling in hurt. The mightiest man of that ancient age
Was gripping Grendel fast in his fist.
No incentive would induce the chieftain's champion
To release his grip on that loathsome guest.
For it was his view that no value attached   90
To so violent a life. That hardened entourage,
The warriors of Beowulf, brandished aloft their seasoned swords.
The best and the bravest, protecting their prince,
Dared to defend the life of their lord.
None of them knew, those tough retainers,   95
When they fell to the fray, at the maddened monster
Seeking to strike, that no bright blade,
Not the sharpest of swords, no edge on earth
Could blood that beast: for he'd bewitched,
From point to pommel, all weapons of war.   100
Yet the point of departure for him drew near,
The hour when this wretch would reach his end;
When his stranger's spirit would be hauled to its home,
Committed to the devilish care of the damned.
This culprit, guilty of so many crimes,   105
Who'd brought so much misery to the minds of men,
And even fought the Almighty Father,

23

Found that his body failed to obey
When he knew that the keenest kinsman of Hygelac
In a duel to the death held him by the hand.   110
Terrible torment felt the fiend in his limb.
In his shoulder sprang open a deep incision:
There was snapping of sinews and breaking of bone.

To Beowulf the victory, the glory was given;
While Grendel fled swiftly, mortally damaged,   115
Seeking the shelter of his fenland lair.
Certain and sure was the creature's conviction
That his death-day had dawned;
While the Danes had achieved all that they'd hoped for
From that fatal fight. The high-hearted hero   120
Who'd hunted and harried so far from his homeland
Had rescued from ruin Hrothgar's hall.
He was pleased with his prowess, took delight in his deeds.
To the Danes he'd delivered, and paid back his promise:
He'd assuaged all their anguish, appeased all their pain;   125
Healed all the heartache, so trying a torment,
They'd earlier endured.

                    And for a memorial
Of that mighty struggle, see, there, the sign:
Grendel's great limb, hoist up by the hero –
Snapped-off and severed, shoulder and shank,   130
Forearm and finger, clutch and claw –
To the beam bolted, roped to the rafters
Of Heoret's cavernous roof.

Beowulf[1] is the single largest poem to survive from Anglo-Saxon
times, and its plot, narrative action, and style are all in keeping
with an expansive, epic scale. The poem begins, as the extract
above indicates, with the origins of the Danish royal house, and
settles on the prosperous reign of Hrothgar (a famous character
in early Scandinavian writings) as the focus of its story. To
celebrate his success Hrothgar builds a great hall, Heorot ('Hart
Hall'), and there rewards and entertains his retinue and their
community. The hall, however, becomes subject to the attacks of
a monstrous creature, Grendel, an outcast who envies humanity
its pleasure and prosperity. Grendel begins to attack the hall,
breaking in and devouring as many as thirty warriors at a time.
Some years of this trial elapse before the young hero Beowulf, of
the tribe of the Geats (a people from the land that became

Sweden) hears of it, and travels to Hrothgar's kingdom to attempt the adventure of dealing with the monster. Beowulf lies in wait for Grendal (Parts XI–XII, above) and fatally wounds the creature with his bare hands.

The remainder of the poem's first half then repeats the story with differences: Grendel's mother emerged from her lair to exact vengeance for her son, and repeats his acts of butchery. Beowulf has to seek her out at the mere where she lives. As he seeks her in the depths, she drags him to the bottom, but his superhuman strength and endurance, together with his fortunate finding of a giant sword, enables him to kill her. At the feast of celebration that follows, the effect of triumph is undermined by narrative allusions to a future in which Hygelac, king of the Geats, will meet disaster. As Fred C. Robinson puts it, it is characteristic of the poem's narrative method to 'leave one with a sense that even the most shining moments in the heroic world are darkened by the prospects of ineluctable tragedies to come and with a sense of fate implacable'.[2]

On his return to Geatland, Beowulf is welcomed and feasted by his king Hygelac, and given the opportunity to recapitulate the whole story of Grendel and his mother. The poem's narrative then breaks and jumps ahead for more than half a century. Hygelac, the poet explains, was later killed, and succeeded by Beowulf, who reigned well for fifty years. A great dragon is woken and antagonized by the stealing of a cup from the treasure-hoard he guards. The dragon devastates the realm, and King Beowulf accepts that he alone is capable of facing it. He goes against the monster with a loyal companion, Wiglaf, and together they manage to kill it. Beowulf, however, has received his death-wound, dies, and is cremated. The poem ends with gloomy predictions of the disasters that will befall the Geats now their king is dead. Beowulf's ashes are interred in a great monument on a cliff-top, together with the treasure from the dragon's hoard.

The poem opens with a call to attention: the word *Hwaet*,[3] usually translated as 'Hear!' or 'listen!', locates the epic in the context of performance described in Chapter 1. The *scop*, or singer, calls for silence, and demands concentrated attention from his audience. He invokes a familiar, shared repertory of narratives within a common culture – 'We've heard' (l. 1). He

25

places the time of his story very definitely in a distant past – *geardagum*[4] – former days; days gone by; ancient times. If we were thinking of *Beowulf* as a 'primary epic', as a poem originating in a society similar to that described in the action, there would still be an emphasis on the past, on the great deeds of the tribal ancestors, on the actions and adventures of men who are always bigger and stronger than those of the present day. However, if we think of the poem in terms of its probable context of composition in a literate and Christian culture, then *geardagum* begins to seem much further back, a society considerably more remote, and to some extent alien; a past which is another country, where they do things differently. 'It is now to us itself ancient', wrote J. R. R. Tolkien of the poem: 'and yet its maker was telling of things already old'.[5] We see a poet writing with some ambiguity of perspective from his culture of laws and charters, monasteries and churches and libraries, a relatively advanced social organization with an established literate culture – and describing the actions of men who live entirely by pre-Christian codes of war-band loyalty and epic heroism.

As in any epic poem, the present of the narrative is contextualized within an antecedent past, as the dynastic history of the Danes is sketched through a genealogical tree. Again, we have no means of knowing whether the poet and his audience were relatively recent settlers in England, who had brought with them a nostalgia for their Scandinavian ancestry, or a tribal or ethnic group which looked back from a later time to more remote, but still revered, Nordic forebears. Some critics have drawn attention to the irony of the historical fact that, during the most likely period of the poem's composition (the ninth or tenth centuries), the Danes were, to the English, hostile invaders, who harried and raided their eastern seaboard. The crafty and bloodthirsty pirates who face Byrhtnoth across the cold waters of the River Panta in the *Battle of Maldon* may have been descendants of the Hrothgar celebrated in the poem.

The account of Scyld Scefing's death and funeral, which marks the point of origin for the Danish royal house, displays a haunting beauty which seems to me to arise directly from the complexities of feeling and belief immanent within a historically transitional, multicultural society. Scyld, founder of the Scylding dynasty, has all the legendary mystery proper to a folk-hero in

such a 'myth of origin'. His name combines the associations of
'shield' and 'sheaf' of corn, suggesting both protection and
prosperity, and since he floats inexplicably into the world of the
Danes, his own provenance is a mystery. Scyld is an ideal hero
and king on the Anglo-Saxon model: one who acquired great
wealth by warfare, securing personal loyalty by his own bravery
and success in battle, and enriching his community with the
spoils of war. Like all such ideal rulers, Scyld is depicted as a
benefactor, a 'generous giver' (l. 43). The manner of his funeral,
launched, like the legendary King Arthur, onto water on a
funeral ship, may be regarded as somewhat unusual, and he has
obviously specifically asked his personal retainers to dispose of
his corpse by these particular rites. Scyld is not cremated, as is
Beowulf at the end of the poem. Nor is he, like the subject of the
Sutton Hoo ship-burial,[6] interred together with his personal
possessions. The idea of death as a journey was clearly common
in Germanic culture as it was among the Egyptians: men were
buried with horses, or chariots, or in a boat or ship. Scyld's
obsequies clearly imitate and reduplicate his origins –

> He went as he came, as abundantly endowed
> In his faring forth as his hoving hither...

                                                            (ll. 52–3)

The grave-goods with which his body is accompanied are those
found by archaeologists in many Anglo-Saxon cemeteries, and
are replicated exactly by the Sutton Hoo burial-ship.

The poet has chosen to construct the narrative of Scyld's
obsequies, it seems to me, in a way that combines pagan and
Christian associations. The narrator's radical uncertainty about
the ultimate destination of Scyld's body lies in a creative tension
somewhere between the certainties of paganism and those of
Christianity about the after-life. Though Scyld is embarking on a
journey to an unknown destination, his last voyage may be
tinged with the same optimism attending his first, when he
arrived, a stranger from an undiscovered country, to find
himself gifted with a life of such promise and success. On the
other hand, the poet comments, with the deep scepticism
unavoidable in any thoughtful view of mortality –

> no-one can tell in absolute truth –
> Neither the crafty counsellor in court,

27

> Nor the brave soldier beneath the blue sky –
> – Who, at the last, unloaded that cargo.

(ll. 61–4)

A Christian reader or listener might well, on the other hand, understand the uncertainty expressed here to relate to the fearful possibilities of Judgement. Scyld in death, according to the poem, *feran on frean waere*,[7] was going into God's keeping. But after all, though a noble and virtuous pagan, Scyld would have lived (if he was a historical rather than a legendary character) in a fourth-century Denmark untouched by the teaching of Christ, and the early Church taught that such heathens were destined to ultimate damnation. Did he live to achieve only worldly renown, that may have been anything but pleasing to the Christian Lord? Or does the poem seek to align the lasting reputation achievable by worldly success with the kind of virtuous record that would win paradise at the end? At the end of the poem Beowulf's soul goes forth in death to seek *soðfaestra dom*[8] ('the reward of the just'). *Dom* ('doom') can mean either 'judgement' or 'glory' (as well as 'choice', 'law', court', 'magnificence', 'reputation' and 'power'!). It was certainly assimilated to Christian purposes in the coinage *domesdaeg*, Day of Judgment. But in the poem's own time it could scarcely have been free from more barbaric associations of worldly, especially military, glory. Beowulf's final epitaph, formulated in the poem's closing lines, seems to mingle the Christian virtues of charity and loving-kindness with a thoroughly pagan hunger for fame:

> He was, they said, among all the world's kings,
> The meekest, the mildest, the gentlest of men,
> Most kind to the nations, most keen for renown.[9]

A similar ambiguity pervades the following sequence, describing the building of Heorot and the social life of the Scylding community. Though (from our modern viewpoint) a monument to plunder and murder, based on expropriated wealth, Heorot becomes in the poem an emblem of the ideal community. The wealth Scyld distributes to his followers is defined not as the wages of rapine, but as the gifts of God (*swylce him God sealde*,[10] 'that which God had granted to him'). Hrothgar's harpist sings not of the heroic deeds of great warriors (as a *scop* later sings about Beowulf's killing of Grendel, Part XIII) but of the Creation

28

of the world. The same word, *fraetwan* (to create, make, shape or build) is used both of the Creation of the world (*gefraetwade foldan sceatas*, 'made the surface of the earth'), and the construction of Heorot (*folcstede fraetwan*, 'to build a hall for the community').[11] The work of God, and the works of man, do not seem in any way dissimilar or incompatible: each creates a small island of order and concord within an unstable world ruled by an amoral *wyrd*.

Beowulf's feat in tackling and destroying Grendel, the monster who ravages Heorot, is typical of combats to be found anywhere in such fantasy epics. It is, at face value, a feat of pure physical strength, as if accomplished by a hero like Hercules. Beowulf's grip is simply too strong for the monster to withstand. At the same time, though Beowulf is no crafty hero in the mould of Odysseus, there is a kind of natural intelligence in his encounter with the creature. He lies quietly in wait; carefully watches the way Grendel attacks; and seems, at least instinctively, to know that only pure strength will avail in this conflict. For Grendel has by some magic spell enchanted all weapons to give himself immunity: Beowulf's retainers strike at him in vain. Beowulf thus pits himself against the evil being in a trial that could, in Christian terms, be seen as emblematic of a trial of faith, like the saint's battle against the fiends in *Guthlac*.[12] Such interpretations can, however, be pushed too far: J. R. R. Tolkien reminds us that abstract ideological interpretation of such a poem runs the risk of killing its imaginative beauty and splendour.[13] In the end what Beowulf accomplishes is a deed from folk-tale and fairy-story: to kill a fearsome monster with his bare hands.

Grendel is perhaps a being of more complexity than the folk-tale narrative of his destruction. He emerges from the darkness of Nordic myth and legend, but is here given very precise Christian definition. He is simultaneously the man-eating troll of Nordic stories, the eerie night-strider of German folk-belief, and a demon, or even the devil, of Christian theology. He is in some ways like a man (he has a soul), and clearly, in his bitter envy of others' happiness, feels a man's emotions; in some ways a kind of phantom or ghost, who steal silently through the darkness and attacks the unsuspecting sleeper. But he is also *feond mancynnes*, the foe of mankind, and an implacable enemy of God. His ancestry lies in the lineage of Cain, the first

29

murderer, and father of all the diabolical enemies of men (ogres and elves), and of God (like the Giants in Genesis 6, who were overwhelmed in the Great Flood).

All these diverse associations are suggested by the poem's description of Grendel, lurking in the darkness, watching the bright light of the hall, envying the security, warmth, and pleasure of its occupants. He is at once a folk-tale monster, arbitrarily and inexplicably hostile to human society; a malicious spectre or phantom, born of the darkness which is always the opposite of light; a tormented exile or outcast, bitterly brooding on his exclusion from social pleasure and community; and perhaps related to Satan himself, as we will find him later dramatized in *The Fall of the Angels* (see below, Chapter 4), cast down from bliss, sworn to a malignant and unappeasable hatred of God and all his works – from the Creation of the world for men to the building by them of Heorot.

THE BATTLE OF MALDON
(ll. 17–113)

Byrhtnoth began	
To draw up his battle-lines, dispose his defences	
And marshal his men. From horseback he exhorted	
And instructed his troops: taught them to stand	
In firm formation; to seize their shields,	5
Fast in their fists; to hold their position,	
And to harbour no fear. Once his warriors	
Were perfectly placed, he dismounted his steed	
And took up his post, there where his loyal	
And loving retainers clustered around	10
Their cherished chief. Then the voice of a Viking,	
Across the wide water, a proud proposition	
Clearly declaimed; to the eminent earl	
As he stood on the strand, the brigands' ambassador	
Brokered a deal: 'The valiant Vikings	15
Have sent me to say that you'll have to pay	
For your own protection. It'll stand you in good stead	
To trade peace for treasure, secure your safety	
With a tribute of rings. It's your only option,	
Cheap at the price – and better by far	20
Than the tough treatment – if it comes to conflict –	

We'll have to hand out. There's no need for brave boys
To kill one another. And if your commander's
Prepared to pay, we're willing to pledge peace
For glittering gold. Come on, fellow-fighters,   25
We'll do you a favour; we'll let you withdraw
And head back to your homes – if you'll only agree
To the terms of our truce. Accept our offer,
Give us the gold, and we'll wrap up our weapons,
Return to our ships, set sail for the flood-ways,   30
And leave you alone.' But that brave Byrhtnoth
Shaking his ash-spear, shouldered his shield
And in rage replied: 'Now hear you, sailor,
What we Saxons say. We'll tender you tribute,
We'll pay you your price; but with seasoned swords   35
And with sharpened spears. This type of tribute
Won't benefit you, when in boisterous battle
You reap your reward. Run away, errand-boy,
And drop this delivery – a word that your warriors
Won't want to hear: here stands a Saxon,   40
Loyal to his liege-lord, ably backed-up
By well-trained troops. We'll defend this domain,
We'll protect our prince; and in love and in loyalty,
For king and for country, keep Aethelred's land.
Expect, pagans, to die on this dirt. We'd never be able   45
To hold up our heads, if you were allowed
To flee unfought, and renew your raids,
Now you've advanced so far on our fields.
And don't think so easily our wealth to acquire
By soft persuasion and weasel words.   50
The axe-edge must arbitrate, the javelin must judge,
Or agreement emerge from the sparring of spears
Before we relinquish our riches to you.'
Then his troops were told
To take their positions, and form a defensive   55
Shield-wall on shore. On both banks the armies
Opposed one another, though anxious and eager,
Unable to engage. For the tide as it turned
Came flowing in flood, and around the island
Its currents closed. Weary of waiting   60
The warriors, impatient, longed with opponents
Their lances to lock. By the ripples of Panta
The East-Saxons stood, the flower of fighting-men
Leaned on their spears. For a stream of safety
Divided them from danger; only the fast flight   65

31

Of a feathered shaft, sprung from a strong bow
Could death deliver. The fast-flowing flood
Ebbed in the estuary, the rippling tide-race
Swept out to sea. The pirates, prepared,
Were keen for the kill. So Byhrtnoth his brave men   70
Quickly commanded the crossing be kept,
The ford defended. A war-hardened warrior,
Wulfstan by name, slew with his spear
The first of the Vikings foolish enough
To step on the ford. Two keen companions   75
Were covering Wulfstan, Maccus and Aelfere,
Two valiant veterans. You wouldn't see them
Take flight at the ford: they'd steadfastly stand
Against an enemy as long as a weapon
They were able to wield. Then those devious vikings,   80
As soon as they saw that the shore-defenders
Would put up a fierce fight in keeping the causeway,
Began to use guile. They asked of the earl
To allow them safe-conduct, to pick them a passage
Over the causeway; across the estuary   85
To advance their troops before the attack,
And re-form by the ford. Eagerly the earl,
In excess of pride, to unwelcome invaders
Began to give ground. Clearly he called
Across the cold water: 'Without fear of affray,   90
Come over the ford: the causeway is clear.
Come quickly to us, and let's meet in the mêlée.
Only the Lord knows whose power and pride
This day will preserve, who will at the last
Be left lord of the field.' Their appetites whetted,   95
Those wolves of war waded through water,
Careless of cold. The viking warriors
Advanced from the east, over the shining stream
Held up their shields, bearing their linden-boards
Safely to shore. Ready for resistance   100
The Saxons stood firm. As their chieftain commanded
They locked their shields, forming a war-wall
Against the fell foe. As the conflict grew closer,
Keen for the struggle, steadfast swordsmen
Scented success, glory of battle   105
Lay in each one's grasp. But every man knew
That a share of those shieldsmen
Were doomed for destruction, marked
For the massacre, fated to fall.

Hubbub of battle loudly arose. Raucous the raven, 110
For carrion circling. Expectant the eagle,
Eager for prey. Earth rang with the uproar.
Then from hard hands flew file-hardened lances,
Savagely-sharpened spearpoints were flung.
Bowstrings were busy, sword struck against shield. 115
Bitter the battle: on all sides
Soldiers were slaughtered, young lads laid low.

As we move from *Beowulf* to *The Battle of Maldon*, we encounter a poem which, although written within very similar conventions and sharing a common and consistent heroic view of life, seems 'modern' and contemporaneous rather than antique, and explicitly historical rather than mainly a matter of myth, legend, and fantasy. It is perhaps important to note that some of these differences may be more a matter of style than of content: it is possible, for example, that the kind of fantasy literature we find in *Beowulf* was at one time a particular way of formulating a historical memory. *The Battle of Maldon* was an authenticated historical event, which occurred in 991. The (apparently misdated) entry for 993 in one version of the *Anglo-Saxon Chronicle* reads:[14]

> Here in this year came Anlaf with 93 ships to Stane [Folkestone] and ravaged the region, and from there went to Sanwic, thence to Gipeswice [Ipswich] and overran the whole area, and then to Maeldune; and against him there came Byrhtnoth the *ealdorman* with his *fyrd*, and fought with him. And the *ealdorman* was killed there, and they commanded the battle-field.

There is no comparable reference to authenticate Beowulf's fight with Grendel. Again, the poem contains sufficient topographical detail for the geographical location of the battle to be established, with some certainty, as having taken place in the estuary of the river Blackwater (then called the 'Panta'), with the East-Saxons drawn up on the south-western shore, and the Vikings established on Northey Island in mid-stream. The phrase *lucon lagustreamas* ('the tide-streams locked', or in my translation 'around the island/The currents closed', ll. 59–60[15]) gives an exact indication of the spot, and the tidal causeway (covered at flood and exposed at ebb-tide) is still, unlike Grendel's mere, there to be seen.

When the scholarly consensus held that *Beowulf* was probably composed in the eighth century, using materials of even greater antiquity, possibly dating from the fifth or sixth centuries, then *Maldon* appeared as an elegant modern pastiche or imitation of an old heroic style, deployed to confer meaning and value on a contemporary conflict. Now the possibility is acknowledged that *Beowulf* and *Maldon* may have been written within as little as fifty years of one another, our sense of the relationship in both poems between the contemporary period of composition, and the past the poems describe, is likely to be rather different. Both poems may, in short, have been written in the same self-consciously antique and retrospective mode.

Both the end and the beginning of *The Battle of Maldon* had been lost before a copy was made in the eighteenth century. The passage translated starts near the beginning of what remains. In the rest of the poem, Byrhtnoth is killed, and dies thanking God for the gifts of his life and praying that his soul may have a safe passage to paradise. Disheartened by the lord's death, a warrior, Godric, flees from the battle, taking Byrhtnoth's own horse, and is quickly followed, first by his brothers Godwin and Godwy, and then by others. According to Offa, who stays at his post, this defection, by splitting the army and breaking the shield-wall, loses the battle. Other members of the *heorðwerod* ('home-troop', personal bodyguard), however, stand fast, remembering their august lineage and the boasts they had made before the battle. They will fight to the death rather than yield, or escape from the field where their lord lies slain. The essential warrior ethic of defiance in the face of defeat and death is expressed, in justly famous lines, by an old soldier, Byrhtwold:

> *Hige sceal þe heardra,   heorte þe cenre,*
> *Mod sceal þe mare,   þe ure maegen lytlað.*

The heart must grow harder, stronger the spirit,
The mind swell in mightiness, as our force fails.[16]

As an *ealdorman* Byrhtnoth's job, like that of a feudal lord after the Norman Conquest, was to administer a particular territory on behalf of the king. He was thus responsible for social organization and for the execution of justice. Historically Byrhtnoth is remembered particularly as a notable benefactor to the church. It was also however an *ealdorman*'s job to secure his territory by military defence. In order to do this he would call on the services of his *heorðwerod,* a kind of personal bodyguard, consisting to some degree of close kinsmen; and of a *fyrd* of troops that could be levied from the region in an emergency situation.

Not much of this historical and sociological detail appears in the poem. Although, as indicated above, the manuscript is damaged so that the beginning and end of the poem are lost, it is hard to imagine *Maldon* ever having dwelt on such mundane and quotidian particularity. The heroic style of the poem makes it difficult to think of these warriors as a kind of early version of the Home Guard: the battle feels, in the poem, more like the *Iliad* than an episode of *Dad's Army*.

The battle, although made concrete in time and space, is also to some degree decontextualized and isolated as an outstanding epic combat. Thus Byrhtnoth is depicted, not as an able civil servant and local philanthropist, but as another Julius Caesar, an ideal leader, the skilful and experienced general who personally instructs his troops in military strategy and tactics. These tactics, however, are essentially defensive: the warriors are lined up, close together, facing the enemy, so that their shields form a defensive wall. The men are exhorted to stand fast, so that any potential frontal assault would be held and hopefully repelled. Satisfied with his tactical preparations, Byrhtnoth dismounts and takes his place together with his personal bodyguard. The Vikings, as was their custom, make an offer of accommodation, demanding what we would now term 'protection money'. If the Saxons are prepared to pay an appropriate and acceptable tribute, they will be left in peace. The objective of the Norse raiders was obviously at this point to acquire wealth by plunder, rather than to overrun the territory by conquest. If the plunder could be obtained without battle and costly loss of life, so much the better. After the battle was lost, the *Anglo-Saxon Chronicle* notes, the tribute (presumably by now considerably inflated at x *þusend punda*) had in any case to be paid.

Although the speech of the Viking messenger is a formal negotiating offer (in the translation, I've used contemporary words like 'broker' and 'deal' to emphasize this aspect), Byrhtnoth does not need to consult with his followers before making an answer. The automatic speech and gesture of heroic resistance is virtually instinctive, expressed as eloquently in the raising of his shield – a call for silence and attention, here obviously a gesture of defiance – as in the speech that follows. Byrhtnoth's speech has all the clarity and simplicity of the heroic ideal. It insults the enemy (which was one of the recognized functions of the formal challenge or *beotword* – Byrhtnoth contemptuously addresses the Viking messenger as *saelida*,[17] 'sailor' or 'pirate'), promises fierce resistance against any attack, and flatly refuses the tribute the raiders request. Although Anglo-Saxon communities frequently did pay tribute to the Vikings, Byrhtnoth talks as if to do so would represent an ineradicable mark of shame and dishonour.

In addition to this reliance on heroic virtue, however, the preference of death before dishonour, Byrhtnoth also invokes the strength of the tight social organization into which this particular section of 'coastal defence' is ultimately locked. As *ealdorman*, Byrhtnoth is loyal to his king, and will defend to the death the king's life and lands. In turn Byrhtnoth's men are loyal to their lord, and suitably qualified and equipped for their task. At the same time, Byrhtnoth gives voice to that fatalistic respect for the chances of battle that sounds strongly in all Old English heroic literature. A man may be bold and resolved, he may fight with courage and determination; but he may, like Beowulf himself, still endure defeat. Such defeat would not, however, undermine the value and significance of his achievement in standing firm and doing his best. There is nothing shameful in the prospect of dying in battle: in fact it may be exactly the way to ensure that one's memory among the living survives to be celebrated and revered. The only shame is in shrinking from combat; the only dishonour the cowardice of taking flight.

However, Byrhtnoth's military strategy, as is appropriate for one of his position and responsibility, is purely defensive. He knows how to stand against an assault and repel it: but he shows no sign of any inclination to attack. The Vikings, for their part, though a raiding-party poised to attack, are prevented from engaging by the barrier of the tidal estuary. This stalemate, or 'Mexican stand-off', continues until the tide recedes and the ford is uncovered by the retreating waters. The Vikings, now resolved on conflict, attempt to enfilade across the causeway. But the narrow ford is easily defended by only three Saxon warriors.

This is the turning-point of the poem, where the action is displaced from history into legend. Clearly the *ealdorman* has done his job: he has effectively defended his position and kept the Vikings contained. In terms of his civic function, nothing more is required of him. But the invaders then make a request that Byrhtnoth allow them to cross the ford and regroup on the southern shore in order that pitched battle may be engaged. The poem uses the word *lytegian*[18] to describe the Vikings' motivation, a verb not used elsewhere but evidently suggesting 'guile', 'cunning', 'deviousness'. This proves something of a problem for interpretation of the poem: for if the Vikings are devious in their request, then Byrhtnoth is gullible in acceding to it. Byrhtnoth allows them to cross, the poem indicates, out of *ofermod*[19] ('excess of pride'): perhaps a reckless appetite for adventure, perhaps a foolhardy taste for suicidal heroics; perhaps even a sporting sense of fair play, such as that shown by Beowulf when he scorns to wear armour to engage with an unarmed enemy, Grendel. It is worth noting that *ofermod* is used of Satan – *se engel ofermodes*[20] – in the poem known as *Genesis A*; so for the Christian reader, one meaning of *ofermod* was certainly that of the fundamental sin of pride.

If the England of 991 was a society which valued peace and stability, a community of 'settlers' (who would wherever possible avoid the disruptive effects of military action), rather than 'raiders' like the Vikings,[21] then a pragmatic and tactically sensible approach to this crisis would have been to retain the military advantage, and prevent the Vikings from coming ashore. Of course, as has been pointed out, the raiders, if repelled, might simply have withdrawn to strike at some other point on the coast, possibly again within Byrhtnoth's own territorial responsibility; so there was a clear advantage in attempting to stop them. On the other hand, as even the most peace-loving of communities usually discovers at some point, it is possible to face a simple choice between military resistance, and subjugation which can entail total destruction. In such a case the heroic military virtues tend to be adopted, even if reluctantly, as something of a necessity. If the East Saxons of 991 did not revere the values of soldiership in quite the same absolute and unconditional manner as did their Germanic ancestors some four or five centuries previously, when faced with the prospect of a Viking invasion, they would obviously have felt a need to rediscover them.

The Battle of Maldon insists unequivocally on the absolute imperatives of courage, determination, and unshakeable loyalty to one's lord. To flee from the scene of a battle, as does Godric, is a humiliating disgrace which ought to make life subsequently intolerable for the coward. The Anglo-Saxon heroic ethic, however, goes further than this, prescribing that it is impossible for a warrior to leave alive a battle-field on which his lord has been slain. The final heroic resistance of Byrhtnoth's *heorðwerod* is therefore in keeping with this conception of heroic virtue. The Roman historian Tacitus in his *Germania*, a description of the Germanic tribes written in the first century AD, states, 'To leave a battle alive after their chief has fallen means lifelong infamy and shame'.[22] We have to assume either that this principle remained fundamentally unaltered for nigh on a millennium; or that in seeking to memorialize a contemporary conflict in an appropriate form the poet reached back to older literary antecedents, possibly even including the works of Tacitus himself. This is perhaps not unusual. Written commentaries on contemporary military actions, even today, often deploy language derived ultimately from the feudal militaristic code of chivalry. On the other hand, it is undoubtedly by this scrupulous adherence to the heroic virtues of loyalty and self-sacrifice that the poem is able to create a miniature heroic epic out of a humiliating defeat. The greatness and dignity of Byrhtnoth's achievement, and the example of his followers, is that they stood firm at their posts and were killed in action. It is a point of honour that Byrhtnoth did *not* seek the kind of pragmatic accommodation that might have saved his own life, and the lives of his men. He was not prepared to accept peace at the price of dishonour. And if it was so imperative to die in battle rather than endure dishonour, then Byrhtnoth's *ofermod* becomes entirely vindicated.

3

Elegiac Poetry

THE RUIN

As well-wrought as this wall was
Fate fractured it, smashed this stronghold.
Toppled towers, ruptured rafters
Rot in rubble. Hail-hammered gateways
Crumble with cold. Ruined roofs –   5
Shattered shower-shields – eaten by age.
Where are the wrights, wielders of wood,
Sculptors in stone? In the grip of the grave,
Gone, long since gone. Deep they decay
While their works wither. This wall weathered   10
The crashing of kingdoms: stood against storms
Where kinsmen clashed in a splintering of spears.
First the factor, skilled with stone
Agile in art, melted metal
To bolster the base. A wonderful work!   15
When it was built, bright was the building,
Gorgeously gabled. Masses of men
Milled in the mead-hall, the row of rioters
Rang through the roof. Thickly they thronged,
Proud in their pleasure, choice in their cheer.   20
But Destiny doomed them,
Dealt them a double blow: pillaged by plague,
Battered by battle, the flower of the folk
Fell. This fort fragmented, and fell to waste,
To rack and ruin. The masons melted away,   25
The valiant men vanished. Hence are these halls
Desolate and dreary: tiles are torn
From the red roof. Decay has devastated,
Reduced to rubble this peerless pile:
Where once, in old days, a host of heroes   30

Happy in heart, and glittering with gold,
Fair and wine-flushed, fed on the sight
Of shimmering silver and joyed in gems.
Ravished by riches, gladdened by gold,
They gazed on the splendour of this bright burg,   35
This celestial city and its circling domains.

The poem we know as 'The Ruin' appears on two badly
damaged leaves of the Exeter Book: so the original comes down
to us, perhaps fittingly, in a dilapidated and fragmentary
condition. Towards the end of what remains of the poem,
some lines describing the miracles of Roman plumbing begin,
and then disintegrate into illegibility; so the translation above is
therefore much neater and more finished than the original
literary document; a modern reproduction of an artistic
construction that appears, in its manuscript form, as to some
degree a ruin of itself.[1]

There are a number of references in Anglo-Saxon poetry to
the surviving ruins of an ancient civilization, obviously the
collapsed remains of Roman occupation. The hero of *The
Wanderer* also describes, and broods over, the remnants of
buildings that seem, in their scale, magnificence, and ingenuity
of construction, to have been *enta geweorc*, the work of giants.[2]
Scholars have tended to speculate that *The Ruin* is based on the
Roman city of Bath, though there would obviously be a number
of other possibilities. Often philosophical and religious conclu-
sions are drawn from the contemplation of such remains; but
this is not the case with *The Ruin*, which operates in a more
concrete, sensuous, and purely poetic way, by dwelling on the
physical details of ancient ruins, and imaginatively reconstructing both the life they contained and the process that brought
them to destruction. More general observations about the
transience of human achievements and the fragility of mortal
existence, that normally feature strongly in other poems, are
absent here. All such implications are left to be inferred from the
evidence, rather than abstracted and formally stated within the
poem. In this way the poet's imagination works backwards from
the physical ruins he describes with such vivid particularity of
detail towards that dark and distant past those ruins now merely
commemorate.

The poem is full of admiration for the constructions of the past, as well as being acutely aware of their fragility. The wall was well-wrought, *wraetlic*,[3] skilfully and ingeniously constructed, before the irresistible power of Fate destroyed it. Right from the outset, then, there is a dual acknowledgement of the power of human achievement, as registered in the creative success of the original architects and builders, and a chastening recognition of the immense destructive force that has caused their work to collapse. In order to capture that sense of loss, which holds together an admiring memory of the past with a saddened resignation at the contemplation of its disappearance, the poet uses a formula common in Latin elegiac poetry, known as the *ubi sunt* motif, from the phrase meaning 'Where are they now?':

> Where are the wrights, wielders of wood,
> Sculptors in stone? In the grip of the grave,
> Gone, long since gone.

(ll. 7–9)

We will encounter the *ubi sunt* technique again, repetitively deployed to form an elegiac song, in *The Wanderer* (ll. 114–28).

In expressing curiosity about where the builders and craftsmen have gone (the answer, since these Roman ruins were centuries old at the time the poem was written, being fairly obvious), the poet is also reflecting on the fact that their skills, ingenuity, and creative potentialities have passed away with them from the earth. Once they were both living and capable of building this great city. Now both the artist and his work, in a close sympathy, have decayed and resolved into corruption. Having established the polarities of his imaginative vision, the decayed present and the brilliant remembered past – within the framework of the great transition from life to death, between creativity and destruction – the poem moves to a consideration of some of the events that have occurred, in the mean time, in the vicinity of the buildings, and which may have made some contribution to its fall.

To the Anglo-Saxon mind, all walls were understood to have been defensive: the narrator of *The Wanderer* contemplates a similar wall, and imagines it as the scene of heroic deeds and of fatal slaughter (ll. 91–4). Many battles have been fought, many kingdoms have risen and declined, within the duration of this

41

monument. The poem then goes back to the origin of the buildings, marvelling at the ingenuity of its engineering. Reconstructing the process of its construction leads the poet to imagination of what it must have been like when new, a scene of communal rejoicing and social pleasure which is clearly drawn from Anglo-Saxon experience rather than historically imagined from any knowledge of Roman times. Like Heorot in *Beowulf*, the building itself becomes a symbol of a vital and prosperous society, confident and successful, expressing in social pleasures the continuous celebration of a community's life together. But that brightly lit building, echoing to the sounds of joyful revelry, is seen, from a great distance, by a poet looking across the darkness of the intervening centuries, almost as Grendel peers from his shadows at the brightness and gaiety of Hrothgar's hall. For that community now has vanished: whether destroyed by war, or by the depredations of disease, the poet does not know. Although those ancient men shed such a bright light over the darkness of the world, their luminosity was no stronger than the life of man, and its duration no longer than the brief span of a people's history. This perspective is illustrated in a well-known passage of Bede's *Ecclesiastical History* where life is compared to the brief flight of a sparrow through a brightly lit hall. In the context of a discussion in the court of King Edwin about the relative merits of pagan and Christian religions, one of the courtiers develops this analogy:[4]

> When we compare the present life of man on earth with that time of which we have no knowledge, it seems to me like the swift flight of a single sparrow through the banqueting-hall where you are sitting at dinner on a winter's day with your thegns and counsellors. In the midst there is a comforting fire to warm the hall; outside, the storms of winter rain or snow are raging. This sparrow flies swiftly in through one door of the hall, and out through another. While he is inside, he is safe from the winter storms; but after a few moments of comfort, he vanishes from sight into the wintry world from which he came. Even so, man appears on earth for a little while; but of what went before this life or of what follows, we know nothing.

Towards the end of *The Ruin*, the poet's eye returns again to the present, and again depicts, in fascinated detail, the past's fragmented physical remains. Once again, however, in the switchback motion that is the poem's essential structural pattern, observation of the present leads to imagination of the past. In the very act of piecing together words and phrases, fragmentary bits and pieces of language, into a design which is capable of filling the imagination with presence and plenitude, the poet fills in the blanks that lie between the scattered pieces of broken brick and masonry, the shattered foundations, the torn roof-tiles. The poem as we have received it, in its strange fragmentary unity, comes to rest not in ruin and darkness, but with a brilliant vision of the ideal Anglo-Saxon community, proud in its pleasures, confident in its wealth, inhabiting a metropolitan cityscape of unimaginable beauty and splendour, the like of which a Scandinavian or Saxon immigrant would be unlikely to have seen outside his imagination (*burh* was the name given to the Late Saxon fortified towns which were extensively built from the late eleventh century onwards, and which were relatively substantial urban centres of trade and population.[5] But the poet of *The Ruin* seems never to have seen anything like the utopian cityscape suggested by these fragmentary remains). Just as the poem, with its intricate design and beautifully achieved structure, shows what can be done by craft and skill in rebuilding the fragments of a language, so the poem's closing vision affirms, against the encroaching darkness and in recognition of the permanence of loss, the brightness and power of human potentiality.

THE WANDERER

'How often a loner longs for the Lord,
Looks for His love, and grasps at His grace;
While heavy in heart, he pushes his prow
Through the ocean's emptiness, heaves with his hands
At the ice-cold oar; in endless exposure   5
To pitiless frost, tearful he travels
The paths of the exile, the wanderer's way.
His fate is fixed, his Destiny determined.'

Such an earth-bound exile, suffering in silence,
Sang of his sorrows in words of woe,   10
Of cruel killings, and the perishing of princes.

'Fate has no mercy. I mourn alone,
Telling myself the tale of my griefs.

43

There's no man alive to whom I may talk
Frankly of my fate, or confess my cares.   15
It's only too true that a man is wise
To trap his thoughts tight in his head,
And fasten his feelings firm in his breast.
A spent spirit can't fight fate.
Hard thoughts don't help. A secret is safe   20
If you keep the key secure in your skull.
So I, sorrow's servant, forlorn of my fatherland,
Fetter my feelings deep in my heart;
Ever since I, in a distant day
Gave to the ground my giver of gold,   25
The lord I loved. Then woeful as winter
I quit his cairn, and committed my keel
To the water's waste. Near and far
Through the world I searched, sick for a home,
Hungry for a hall: wanting only one   30
To befriend me, friendless, one wistful to wind me
In welcoming arms. You have to have known
How bitter it is – when care's your companion,
Forlornness your friend – to open your eyes
On no green field, or forge-bright gold;   35
But on foreign faces, and hostile hearts.
Cruel memory calls then to mind,
In the milling mead-hall, the granting of gifts
From the gold-giver's grace; how in years of his youth
His loving lord embraced his loyalty,   40
And joyed him with gems. But that glee's all gone.
The man who's lost the cheerful counsel
And cherishing love of a charitable host,
Harbours a hurt that hits him hard.
When sleep and sorrow, subtly linked,   45
Lull the loner in deception of dreams,
His fantasy fills with voiceless visions
Of the love he's lost. He kens that he kisses
His loved liege-lord; with head and hands
Caresses his knee; remembers the rites   50
Of gift and service, the endless exchanges
Of loyalty for love. But when he awakes
To the yellow waves, and glimpses the gulls,
Fanning their feathers in baths of brine,
It's snow he sees, and hostile hail.   55
Sorer then still is the heart's hurt,
When musing memory calls to mind

Kind company, the sweetness of speech
From loyal lips. But those palpable pleasures
Are deluding dreams, that melt into mist   60
And sink without trace, leaving no sign
On the sea's surface. Surges
Of sadness constantly assail
He who must steer on the icy ocean
His cold and aching heart.   65
So why in the world should I not
Despair, and my heart grow
Dark with the northern night sky's
Annunciation of snow, when I see
Peerless princes, royal retainers,   70
Such valiant men so suddenly vanish,
The homesteads vacated, voided the halls?
Between heaven and hell, this whole middle-earth
Moults and moulders, withers and wanes.
You have to have had your fair share of winters   75
In this whitening world, before you can call yourself
Worldly wise. Wisdom is patient, long-suffering,
Keeps control of its speech, bears and believes
And endures all things. Wisdom is neither
Recklessly rash, nor faltering in fight;   80
Not avid for glory nor greedy for gold;
Neither too careless, nor too concerned.
With wisdom the wise see the world
As it is. Wisdom will wait
Before voicing a vow, till the mind's crystal clear   85
In purpose of action. Wisdom knows well
What a dreadful place this world will be
When all of its wealth stands waste;
As we see every day, every where,
Such ruinous remnants of spent splendour   90
As the windswept wall of a broken
Building, tattered by tempests
And fringed with frost. And though, by that wall,
Daring defenders, vaunting in valour,
Protected their prince, in their pride they perished   95
And fell at its foot. Deprived of delight,
Now they lie with their liege-lord, while the mead-hall
Quietly moulders in the rubble of its ruin.
Nearer and nearer the halls of unhappiness,
By different directions each one draws.   100
One took his leave at the edge

45

Of the axe. One was borne by a bird
On the ocean's waves. One
Found his way to the realm of the joyless
By the grey wolf's jaws; and another   105
Enveloped in earth by a sad-faced friend.
So in the past, the ancient Architect
Annihilated this earth, till the inhabitants
Lay drowned and deep, the edifices of elders
Destroyed, desolate and destitute of revelry.   110
Now, having brooded on this broken wall,
And carefully considered its fragile foundation;
Deliberated on death, and the darkness of life;
Thoroughly thought through this empty existence –
My heart has the wisdom to sing this song: 115

Alas! for the day
Of the horse and the hero,
Alas! for the lord's
Hospitable hall;
Alas! for the bright cup   120
With wine overflowing
Alas! for the loss of it all.

Where now can we find
The joys of the mead-hall?
The splendour of princes,   125
The glory of kings?
To darkness departed,
And under night's helmet
Vanished, as if
There were never such things.   130

Now this broken bulwark, this high wall,
Still wonderfully wrought, pointed and patterned
With the sea-snake's insignia, elaborately
Carved in its crafted coils, is memory's monument
To that honourable host, that fellowship felled   135
By the gore-greedy spear's irresistible strength,
And by infamous Fate's irrefutable force.
Now storms strike the stonewall, and whirlwinds of snow
Worry and whiten the soil. Winter's on its way.
Black night-shadows hurry from the north,   140
With the unfriendly force of hostile hail.
Invincible Fate's iron hand
Keeps its grip on man's little kingdom,

46

And all is hardship here under heaven.
We bring nothing into this world of woes   145
And we take nothing out. Nothing lasts long:
All is always forever lost, land and loyalty,
Kith and kin. In the last days
All of the earth will be empty and desolate,
Dark and deserted; even the high wall   150
For all its antiquity, finally fallen.'

These were the words, the words of the wise man,
Withdrawn to contemplation, searching his heart:

'Blessed the man
Who keeps his faith firm, and never reveals   155
Tormenting thoughts, till a certain remedy's
Ready to hand. Blessed the man
Who hungers for grace; who longs
For the love, and craves for the comfort
Of the Father in heaven. All succour,   160
All safety, all certainty, all love
Lie only with Him, our only
Assurance. He is our haven; He
Is our home.'

The Wanderer,[6] like its companion piece *The Seafarer,* is a dramatic monologue with an intensive focus on the psychological suffering and existential anguish of an exile. Scholars have argued about whether the whole poem is the utterance of one speaker, or a number of speakers, or the joint delivery of a narrator and a speaker in dramatic dialogue. However, the narrative and dramatic structure of the poem, though subtle, is not complex or elaborate, and because the expressions of psychological anguish merge naturally into broader meditations on the fragility of human life, even those passages of apparent narrative commentary (such as ll. 9–11) could be conventional pieces of self-reflection (the speaker talking about himself in the third person), rather than an external narrative frame. Simply punctuating the poem differently (it has no punctuation in its manuscript form) would attribute lines differentially to the speaker and the narrator. Equally, the whole poem could be read as spoken by a single complex voice, which moves in and out of dramatic soliloquy, narrative framework, and general meditative reflection.

47

The Wanderer operates on a similar principle of contrast to that employed in *The Ruin*, between a radiant lost past and a painful and despairing present. The climatic extremities of ice and frost, hail and snow, a northern sky perpetually threatening thunderous darkness, are polarized against the vividly recalled happiness of social relationships, the painfully remembered pleasures of communal joy. Where in *The Ruin* the awareness of desolation and the sense of loss are embodied in the fragments of a lost civilization, here in *The Wanderer* they are initially internalized within the body and spirit of the exile, 'felt in the blood and felt along the heart',[7] and then located in a parallel focus on a symbolic ruin.

The poem sites its expressions of psychological anguish and its meditation on the emptiness of all human hope in two adjacent landscapes: one is the sea, always in Anglo-Saxon poetry the exile's surrogate home; the other a scene reminiscent of *The Ruin*, a demolished building that provokes similar reflections on the transience of worldly achievement. In this poem the collapsed building, with its still-standing wall, again merges the diverse associations of Roman civilization and the Anglo-Saxon community. The wall, described as 'wonderfully wrought, pointed and patterned/With the sea-snake's insignia, elaborately/Carved in its crafted coils' (ll. 132–4), looks very much like a Roman ruin; whereas the earlier description of the devastated building identifies it as a *winsalo*, ('mead-hall', l. 97) (which may, on the other hand, simply be the poet's way of describing the remains of Roman civilization).[8]

The speaker of the poem has been forced into exile, certainly by the death of his lord (ll. 24–6), and probably by the annihilation of his community, in a scenario comparable to those anecdotes of a destroyed people that we find at ll. 70–2 and 93-6. We don't of course know exactly why he's an outcast, since he is careful not to reveal his 'secret' (l. 20) even to the reader (he may shamefully have survived his lord and his kin in a battle in which he would rather have died). The poet's imagination is not, however, concerned with the antecedent causes of exile; rather with depicting the exile's world of rejection and isolation, and his psychological landscape of loneliness and despair.

In this poem the present is always cold, dark, fast in the grip of some enormous northern winter; the past is warm, bright, filled with generosity and affection. There is also a future of tenuous hope, which in the course of the poem shifts from a desire to find another worldly home (ll. 28–32), to a yearning for the more permanent home of God's eternal love. As in *The Ruin*, the polarities of past and present alternate, the one modulating into the other like a musical sequence of harmonies and discords. Thus the wanderer wakes each day from luminous and brightly coloured dreams of green fields and shining gold, to the monochrome and inhospitable environment of his present exile; and the sight of that landscape of deprivation, in turn, provokes memories of its opposite, that past in which he participated fully in the reciprocal social relationships of his community, receiving gifts from his lord in exchange for the loyal services he had rendered.

Lines 42–62 repeat the same movement, describing the vividly deceptive dreams in which the exile thinks himself once again back in his vanished past, again embedded in the physical intimacies and social rituals that formed the infrastructure of social cohesion:

> He kens that he kisses
> His loved liege-lord; with head and hands
> Caresses his knee; remembers the rites
> Of gift and service, the endless exchanges
> Of loyalty for love.

(ll. 48–52)

Awaking to the discomfort and privation of the empty sea, he sees in place of the presences that filled his dream – the hall, the hall-companions, his loved lord and the gifts of his generosity – only the yellow waves, the gulls, the snow, and the hail.

From l. 66 the poet begins to broaden his vision from the focus on individual suffering, and to extend the perspective of his own misery from dramatized personal pain to a larger, existential despair. By ll. 66–74 the individual bereavement, the loss of a lord, has widened into an elegiac reflection on the inevitable loss, by death, of all such leaders, and the perpetual process of mortal transience. All men in this sense are destined to become wanderers; since no lord lives for ever, no community can guarantee perpetual security and protection:

So why in the world should I not
Despair, and my heart grow
Dark with the northern night sky's
Annunciation of snow, when I see
Peerless princes, royal retainers,
Such valiant men so suddenly vanish,
The homesteads vacated, voided the halls?
Between heaven and hell, this whole middle-earth
Moults and moulders, withers and wanes.

(ll.66–74)

The wanderer's own particularity of suffering has become the condition of the whole human world, this *middangeard*,[9] this 'middle-earth' (l. 73). Lines 75–86 then dwell on the kinds of moral strength and stoic endurance required to sustain life and hope in the midst of this universal decay and despair. The passage is interesting, since it recommends certain values that would have been perfectly at home within a pre-Christian context of Germanic culture: maturity; patience; thoughtful and considerate speech; clarity and determination of purpose. These are also, however, merged with principles that seem to belong more naturally to Christian ethics – courage, but carefully checked by prudence; restraint or even renunciation in the appetite for glory and gold.[10] 'The wise see the world /As it is' (ll. 83–4). But is that 'wisdom' to be understood primarily as pagan stoicism, or as Christian patience? Is the world a place which is simply likely to provide more sorrow than joy, or one which cannot be trusted to deliver any lasting satisfaction or reward?

So far I have discussed the poem as addressing the situation of the individual exile, who has lost his lord, and has possibly seen his kin slaughtered; for whom all happiness and pleasure lie in an irrevocably lost past; and who sees the world as a topography of desolate seas and ruined buildings, a landscape coloured by a permanent winter of the mind. But by the time we reach l. 86 the individual predicament has become a universal condition. We are no longer looking at one man who happens to have encountered misfortune and unhappiness, but at a world in which loss, the death of aspiration, the decay of all hope is the normal condition. The vestigial ruins of Roman occupation are extrapolated (ll. 89–93) into a universal vision of the Last Judgment, when the whole earth will be destroyed to make way for a new (as the first created world was destroyed in the Great Flood, ll. 107–10). Under the pressure of deep-rooted Christian doctrines, the poem is here beginning to essay a radical questioning of the pagan inheritance of Anglo-Saxon culture. For if the ultimate end of all human achievement, even the construction of a great public building like Heorot in *Beowulf*, comes to nothing, then what lasting value can finally be attributed to such activities? Similarly, the image of the warriors, valiantly and courageously defending the wall, is seen in the perspective of their heroic death; but also of the ultimate destruction of the defensive bulwark they symbolically died for. The poem continues to pay its respects to the past, both its impressive monuments and its heroic achievements. But the conclusion it ultimately draws is that all such achievements are destined to an ultimate oblivion. The importance, in pagan culture, of a man's securing an enduring memory after his death, achieved by notable action and transmitted from generation to generation, almost a type of after-life, is fundamentally questioned here, since no-one now remembers who those defenders were, or even what they were defending.

This give us an insight into another aspect of the Anglo-Saxon elegiac form, which laments not just the loss of security, love, and pleasure, but the passing of the very historical culture within which such experiences were formulated, recorded, and memorialized. This point comes across very strongly in ll. 138–44. There is a chilling finality about the vision in this passage of a world over which a remorseless destiny is inexorably tightening its grip, as the cold and darkness of winter inevitably overwhelm the earth, seemingly adumbrating some great final cataclysm. What the poet derives from an honest facing of that harsh reality is not, however, despair, but wisdom and a gift of song. That which is lost, the pagan world itself, can be appropriately and movingly lamented in a formal elegy, which is marked off from the narrative by an introductory statement 'My heart has the wisdom to sing this song':[11]

> Alas! for the day
> Of the horse and the hero,
> Alas! for the lord's
> Hospitable hall;
> Alas! for the bright cup

With wine overflowing
Alas! for the loss of it all.
Where now can we find
The joys of the mead-hall?
The splendour of princes,
The glory of kings?
To darkness departed,
And under night's helmet
Vanished, as if
There were never such things.

(ll.116–30)

But that is not the end of the story. This is not the only poetic medium the poet is able to command. For he has also learned, from experience and meditation, another poetic language, derived from another belief-system, and with it another basis for hope. Hence the poem ends with a Christian prayer, again differentiated as a formal 'poem-within-a-poem'. The wanderer has at last found another lord, another allegiance, another home:

'Blessed the man
Who keeps his faith firm, and never reveals
Tormenting thoughts, till a certain remedy's
Ready to hand. Blessed the man
Who hungers for grace; who longs
For the love, and craves for the comfort
Of the Father in heaven. All succour,
All safety, all certainty, all love
Lie only with Him, our only
Assurance. He is our haven, He
Is our home.'

(ll.154–64)[12]

THE SEAFARER

My self's own story I truthfully tell,
My traveller's tale, how day after day
In dark of despair I endlessly endured
Heartache's hurt on the water's waste,
Surges of sadness on weltering waves.   5
Void were my vigils at the mast's foot,
Waste the night-watches, when my boat was battered
And tossed against cliffs. My feet were frozen,

Fettered with frost, cramped with cold;
In the ache of anguish, hot was my heart.   10
Keen as a knife, desire drew inwards
To stab at my soul. Those living on land
Who prosper in plenty amongst fair fields,
Can't possibly know of the poor man's pain,
Who woeful as winter – forlorn of his fatherland,   15
Kept from his kin – weathers the waves
Of the ice-cold sea. Hammered by hail,
Savaged by snow, my ears heard only
The sound of the sea, splash of the surge
And the swan's song. The clamour of gulls   20
My only glee; the call of the curlew,
No man's mirth; the mew's plaint
In place of mead. Where storms beat on stone-cliffs
The icy-winged eagle and frost-feathered tern
Compete in their clamour. There's no loving lord   25
To embrace the exile, or fondly befriend,
With outstretched arms, the friendless man.
A life of luxury's made for that man
Who sojourns in cities, caressed with comforts
And warmed with wine. He feels not a fraction   30
Of the seafarer's sorrow, the hateful hardships
An exile endures. He'll never know,
That creature of comfort, how some of us suffer
On this vast voyage. Darkness deepens
With drifts of snow, shadows of night   35
Bring sleet from the north. Hail falls hard.
Frost grips the ground.

And so my heart heaves to wander the waves,
The unplumbed oceans, and taste of the tang
Of the salt-sea's spray; to seek the deep streams   40
And their restless rolling. There I might seek
Friendship in foreign lands, there I might find
Homeless, a home on an alien shore.
Again and again an impulse invites me,
A peregrine urge to fare far forth;   45
A mood of migration irks me to travel
The pilgrim's passage, the wanderer's way.
No-one in this world is so haughty in heart,
So generously gifted, nor so peerless in pride,
So daring in deeds, nor so loved of his lord   50
That he feels no fear before he embarks,

Of what will befall him on the far seas:
What seafarer's lot the Lord holds in store.
He hears no harping, sees no bright hall,
No place of pleasure. Hollow his heart,   55
And drained of desire; vacant and void
Is the spirit that's set on the traveller's trail,
The mind that's fixed on the whelming waves.
Blossoms burst, fields grow fair,
Forests flourish, the country quickens.   60
All motions move the stirring spirit
To prepare for departure, and fathom the flood.
The cry of the cuckoo, singer of spring,
Brings sharp sorrow to the sailor's breast.
Only the longing of seafaring lasts: 65
The hunger of a heart that desires the deep.
So, stirring, my spirit raps at my ribs,
Flutters her feathers, then quits her cage
To soar on the wing, to fathom the flood-ways,
The earth's expanses, the haunts of the whale.   70
Wheeling and hovering, my heart's hawk yells,
Eagerly inciting the unappeased spirit
To seek the sea's stretches, where the dead lie deep.
Then circling, homing, my falcon stoops,
Repossesses her perch, full of fierce feelings   75
Of desperate desire: longing for Love she is,
Greedy for Grace. See, then, why God's gifts
Mean more to me than the petty pleasures
Of this little life! I can see clearly
That no human happiness endures for ever.   80
There are three deaths, that till destiny's day
Stand still in doubt: illness, old age,
The sword's sharp edge. Each of these snatches at
Life unsuspecting, dreaming of new dawns,
Doomed to depart. What's said after   85
By still-speaking tongues is a man's memorial:
It's memory that matters. So strive to accomplish
Actions of worth, do down the devil
And confound your foes, that your meed may be sung
By the sons of men, and echoed by angels   90
As high as the heavens. For ever and ever,
As life eternal, your fame will be found
In the heavenly host. Dead are the days
Of ancient magnificence, the glories are gone
That once were on earth. No more do we see   95

Caesars and kings, those givers of gold
Who were hailed as heroes, and loved as lords.
They depart into darkness, earth knows them no more.
The great men have gone, their empire on earth
The weak have inherited: men insignificant 100
Cling in their comfort to the world's wealth.
Gone is all glory, all splendour spent,
All empire interred. Antique nobility
Droops and decays. Time's always moving
On this middle-earth. A man ages: 105
Gaunt and grey-haired, he dreams of departed
Days when his loved lord graced him with gifts;
He remembers the royalty of that peerless patron,
Given to ground now, enveloped in earth.
The spirit's sanctuary is fragile flesh 110
That melts in mortality, crumbles to clay.
When life leaves that flesh-house, all bodily being –
Pleasure's sweet taste, the torment of pain,
The touch of a hand, the hastening of thought –
Snuffs out like a flame. A man may hoard 115
In hidden heaps, a trove of treasure
To safeguard his soul; bereaved, a brother,
Broken with grief, will bury bright gold
In his brother's grave, hoping to light him
On his shadowy way. But what good's gold 120
To the sinful soul, when empty-handed
It goes before God? The wealth of the world's
Too poor a price, to placate and pacify
That awful power. Great is the glory,
The grandeur of God. Though He fixed the foundations, 125
Established the earth, the seas and the sky,
Yet will the world fall down before Him
In fear of His wrath. If a man doesn't know
When his death will arrive, unannounced, unexpected,
Like a thief in the night, he's a fool not to feel 130
A dread of the Lord. Blessed the man
Who's humble in heart, for the Lord's mild mercy
Will melt in his soul. Blessed the man
Who holds his faith firm: his fate is forgiveness;
   His gift will be Grace. 135

Although *The Seafarer*[13] displays so many similarities with *The Wanderer*, its structure is substantially different: so much so that editors have been reluctant to accept it as a consistent and

55

continuous dramatic monologue, and have attempted to identify within the poem the presence of more than one speaker.[14] My view is that the poem is, in this respect, no different from *The Wanderer*; and that the apparently contradictory impulses and incompatible ideas we find in it are all part of a single, complex account of a deep spiritual crisis.

The difficulty the poem presents (and in this respect it can be differentiated from *The Wanderer*) is that the situation of exile is regarded from two almost opposite points of view. The poem begins in almost the same way as *The Wanderer*, with a description of the privations and the psychological suffering of an exile; and employs the same polarities as the other poem, comparing a miserable present with a bright, regretted past. But *The Seafarer* reaches the point of Christian resignation, the recognition that mortal life can offer nothing of any enduring value by comparison with the eternal promise implicit in the love of God, much more quickly than does *The Wanderer*; and then goes on to formulate, in poetic and imaginative terms, a spiritual aspiration which offers to lift the soul free from the tangling complexities of a miserable and unpromising world.

The spiritual hunger for an eternal world is symbolized, however, by the same metaphor as is the experience of exile: that of a sea-voyage. It is possible to see here why editors, in search of consistency of character or ideas, have found some difficulty in reconciling the poem's different elements, and have sought to attribute sentiments to different speakers. For one minute the poem is emphasizing exile on the sea as the characteristic location of human suffering; the next minute, expressing an urgent longing to undertake a sea voyage that will ultimately restore the seafarer to his true and only home.

As in *The Wanderer*, the sea is the scene of the seafarer's ordeal. We know even less about the causes of this man's exile than we know of the wanderer's; his situation of dispossession is simply stated and described. The piercing 'desire' that strikes inwards towards the narrator's heart or spirit (*hungor innan slat*),[15] is at first unspecified, suggesting the various possibilities of regret for the past, envy of others' present happiness, or an unappeasable yearning for the hoped-for future. Nostalgic longing for a lost past is the common preoccupation of all the elegies. But *The Seafarer* introduces a different concern, by

56

focusing on the exile's awareness that there are others who, unlike him, still enjoy present pleasure. The emphasis here is on the ignorance and lack of sympathetic awareness he assumes in such fortunate people. This suggests to me that, already, a Christian concern with the limitations of worldly advantages is beginning to make itself felt in the poem – the kind of secure and pleasurable life the exile regrets is to some degree compromised by the observation that such beneficiaries of good fortune are likely to remain insensitive to the miserable plight of the dispossessed and wretched of the earth.

The polarity between past pleasure and present pain is reinforced by a series of ironic comparisons: in place of the happiness, mirth, and feasting of the mead-hall, the exile hears only the harsh and raucous cries of sea-birds, which reinforce his loneliness by mocking the sounds of human company. The seafarer is a typical Anglo-Saxon exile in that he has apparently lost his lord, and presumably also his other friends; and he feels keenly the deprivation of a life without comfort or luxury. But the lack of any explanation of his predicament, and the profound sense of difference and otherness from those who still occupy and enjoy 'normal life', bring into focus the idea of the exile as a universally representative figure, eloquent of a general existential condition of isolation and deprivation.

The deepening winter of ll. 34–7 seems to presage some ultimate climatic catastrophe, some global and glacial disaster, some ice-age of the soul. It is from the hardship and unhappiness of this doomed world that the seafarer is determined to escape. His aspiration is formulated, as I have indicated above, as another sea-voyage. But this is either a journey across a very different sea – an ocean of the spirit, rather than the literal waters that encircle the globe – or it is simply a comparable voyage, conceived in terms of a very different sense of purpose and meaning, and approached from a completely different perspective. For this voyage is not a voyage of exile and escape, not a negatively conceived flight from unhappiness to even greater misery; but a voyage of discovery, a journey of value and purpose. It may even be legitimate to define the journey as a sort of pilgrimage, since the poet begins here to use formal Christian vocabulary. For though the poet speaks of the new journey's object as the discovery of another home, and of the friendship of new companions, this is no ordinary journey from one land to another; nor is its destination a restoration in another form of the community to which the seafarer has bidden a final farewell. This is a journey into uncharted waters, towards an undiscovered country, and in search of a destination unknown. The seafarer knows full well that the home he is seeking is to be found in alien territory, on a distant and foreign shore, beyond the limits of his present society, or even beyond the boundaries of mortal existence.

There is certainly anxiety entailed in this embarkation: not because the direction or destination of the voyage is in any doubt, but because no man can ever be absolutely certain as to how his soul will be judged by the Lord. Even one who, by the worldly standards of his society, may be regarded as preeminently noble and successful – one who is gifted with wealth, confident in his pride, famed for courageous deeds, and strongly protected by a loving lord – can derive no particular confidence from those achievements, since they may have little or no value when brought under the terrible judgment of the Christian God. For this reason, the familiar worldly desires and aspirations for the joys of the hall necessarily fall away from the pilgrim's imagination:

> He hears no harping, sees no bright hall,
> No place of pleasure. Hollow his heart,
> And drained of desire; vacant and void
> Is the spirit that's set on the traveller's trail,
> The mind that's fixed on the whelming waves.

In this remarkable passage we find a virtually complete reversal of the normal priorities of Anglo-Saxon elegiac poetry: for instead of expressing regret for the loss of worldly pleasures, and arriving, in a mood of disenchantment, at the need for an other worldly religious faith, here the paramount importance of spiritual aspiration leads to a voluntary renunciation of conventional worldly longings and desires. Not only does the seafarer cease to regret the loss of such earthly pleasure; he also gives up any wish to regain them. Earthly pleasures and benefits are ascetically subordinated to the fostering of a spirit ready for withdrawal from the world.

In the space cleared by this renunciation of traditional Anglo-

Saxon society's principal values, a new spiritual growth is enabled to develop, beautifully expressed in images of spring-time growth and development:

> Blossoms burst, fields grow fair,
> Forests flourish, the country quickens.
> All motions move the stirring spirit
> To prepare for departure, and fathom the flood.

Such uses of natural imagery to express spiritual awakening became widespread in mediaeval literature (a particularly well-known example is the opening of Chaucer's *Canterbury Tales*). The Anglo-Saxon poem, however, still remains to some extent poised between two worlds: there is regret in this renunciation as well as hope; a painful sense of loss, coexisting with a joyful expectation of the future. The song of the cuckoo, herald of spring, paradoxically sounds a note of sadness, since, for the Christian, springtime means departure from the land that is manifesting these signs of abundance and fertility, and the seafarer is bidding a sad farewell to the natural world from which his metaphors of spiritual regeneration are derived.

His spirit, symbolized in the passage that follows in the metaphor of a falcon, is already ahead of him, driven by a keen migratory impulse from its confinement in his breast (the Latin word *peregrinus*, used to identify a species of hawk – peregrine falcon – means literally 'wanderer' or 'pilgrim'). Through the eyes of that disembodied spirit, as in a 'near-death experience', the narrator is able to secure a lofty aerial perspective on both his present life, clinging timidly to the edge of the land, and the vast seas of infinity that roll perpetually ahead of him and draw him onwards towards them. Death is inevitable: and the fear of death undermines human happiness. Nothing in life, then, can equal the 'joy unspeakable' (1 Peter: 8) that the Christian can find in God's eternal love.

Moreover, since death can arrive with arbitrary and un-expected suddenness, a man must at every moment look to the condition of his soul. Interestingly, this is expressed initially in terms of the traditional pagan conception of a good and enduring memory. A memory, carefully preserved and trans-mitted by affectionate family, or by respectful warrior compa-nions and enemies, was of the first importance to the Germanic pagan. Christianity accepted this deep-rooted premise, and simply encouraged men to leave behind them a reputation for piety, saintliness, and deeds of charity rather than the heroic nobility of a proud and noble name. For example, Byrhtnoth, hero of *The Battle of Maldon*, was obviously careful to cover both these options: a substantial monastic literature celebrates his defence of, and support for, the church; while his martial achievements were celebrated in such epitaphs as the poem, and in a tapestry woven by his wife, Aelflad, which memorialized the great deeds he had accomplished.[16]

The poet of *The Seafarer* subtly merges the pagan conception of a good posthumous reputation with the kind of fame attaching to saints and martyrs, likely, therefore, to be celebrated not only by surviving men and women, but by the angels of God's heavenly host as well. In this context, active resistance to the devil becomes more heroic than the slaughter of mere human enemies. The poem then temporarily returns to the traditional pagan world the poet is explicitly determined to renounce and leave for ever, in one of its most moving and beautiful passages, a formal elegiac lament for the passing of such magnificence, the great kings and emperors of the past, their wealth and their glory. Thus when the image of the exile burying his dead lord returns towards the end of this passage, it is the entire glory of Germanic pagan culture that is being interred and mourned.

Clearly, however, there is no going back. At ll. 115 the poet comments on the continuing practice of burying useful or precious objects together with an inhumed corpse. Where in Germanic tradition it was believed that the body and spirit continued in some mysterious way to survive together, so that the various implements, articles of currency, and vehicles of transport that were inhumed with the dead would remain somehow useful, Christian teaching showed clearly that in death the spirit leaves its *flaeschoma* ('body'),[17] and takes its departure from the shores of this mortal world. An Anglo-Saxon man, devastated by the death of his brother, in a desperate attempt to assist his passage to the otherworld, deposits grave-goods with his body, against the Church's teaching. But his brother, like all men and women, is on his way to appear as a naked soul before the terrible Judgment-seat of God, where worldly wealth will avail him not at all.

4

Christian Poetry

THE DREAM OF THE ROOD

For the Church of St Michael and All Angels, Bedford Park

The day's deep midnight, once it was,
When all earth's creatures' exhausted eyes
Closed, and sleep their shadows shrouded.
Then night's vast womb a dream delivered:
The fairest of all fantasies. An astounding structure   5
I seemed to see soar in the sky,
Its beams bathed in the brightest of light.
Gleaming gold enveloped that vision:
A scatter of jewels sparkled on its shaft,
Yet brighter the stones that encrusted its cross-beam.   10
This was no gangster's gallows, no cross for a criminal:
For all Creation's creatures, all sons of soil,
And a heavenly host of all God's angels,
In beauty of paradise perpetually bright
Admired eternally this vision of victory,   15
This cross of conquest, that triumphal tree.
I was smeared with sin, diseased
With gangrene of guilt, foul with my faults;
Yet I saw this wondrous work, gay and glorious
With glimmering gold, joyfully jewelled,   20
Shimmer in splendour: the cross of Christ.
Still through the gold my eyes descried
An ancient injury, the world's first wound,
Purple on gold, the passion and the glory,
As blood broke forth from the rood's right side.   25
Pierced with pity, and filled with fear
I was, as I saw that shifting sign
Alter its appearance, its colour change:

Now it was wet with the sweat of agony,
Now with brilliance of treasure bedecked.   30
A long while I lay, struck to my soul,
Saddened at the sight of the Saviour's tree;
But imagine the wonder, when this wood
Words uttered, silence broke, spoke
To me!

        'From time's dark backward   35
And abyss, I imagine the hour of my hewing,
When from the wood's end my trunk was toppled,
Wrenched from its roots by the fiercest of foes.
With power they impounded, and made me a spectacle,
A picture of punishment, to rack and to crack   40
The ribs of their criminals. On their shoulders they hefted me,
And on a hill hoisted.
It was then that I saw a splendid Saviour
Approach with alacrity and courage to climb.
Hastily, the young hero stripped Him   45
For action, girded like a gladiator
Ready for the ring. In the sight of spectators,
Fearless and firm, keen for the combat,
He clambered on the cross. He sought no insignia
Of cruel conquest, no brows bound   50
With victorious wreaths: His reward
Was mankind's Redemption, salvation of souls
His only prize. Though all earth faltered
And flinched with fear, I didn't dare
To bend or to break. I'd have fallen full-length,   55
Flat to the earth, but was forced to stand firm.
I could have crushed each of those enemies,
But by Christ's command I had to stand fast.
With shocks I shuddered, when the warrior wound
His strong arms about me: but I daren't stir.   60
More forbidding than fear was the Lord's Word
Crude and rough-hewn, a cross of wood I was:
Yet I lifted on high the Lord of Hosts;
I held aloft the might of majesty. Black nails
Battered through me, opening wide   65
The wounds of wickedness. When they scoffed
At the Saviour, their spit spattered
Me. In His blood when it sprang
From His side, was my splintered surface
Soaked. In the thrust of a spear   70

Was His spirit's expense, when all
Was accomplished, when life He relinquished,
And gave up the ghost. A fearful fate
I endured on that high hill,
A dreadful destiny. I saw the Almighty   75
In agony racked, the corpse of the Ruler
Concealed in clouds. Darkness eclipsed
The original brightness, shadows buried
The Light of the World. All Creation wept
At a King's killing; all creatures cried   80
For Christ on the cross.
A rich man, a follower, arrived from afar,
And begged God's body. Uncertain, anguished,
Humbled with hurt, I surrendered the Saviour
To his outstretched arms. They took Him up   85
Tenderly, torn from His torture,
Left me blood-boltered, impaled by the points
Of annihilating nails. They stretched out His limbs,
Wounded, war-weary; stood at his head,
To say their good-byes; grieved at his going,   90
They laid the exhausted hero to rest.
Full in the sight of me, His murderer,
A tomb they constructed, hewn from bright rock,
Sculpted in stone; and there they interred
The God of glory. A mournful hymn   95
They voiced at evensong; and as darkness deepened
Reluctantly departed. They left Him
Alone there: He needed no companions.
We too were left, three crosses stark
Against an anguished sky: three gaunt gallows   100
On a hill of skulls. The long day waned:
Shadows chilled. In the cool of evening
The Saviour stiffened. For a second time
They savagely felled me, ripped up my roots,
Cruelly cast me in a deep pit.   105
Earth closed coldly over my eyes, eyes
That had seen God's dying. Days,
Years passed: and I perceived only
Comfortless clay, and the darkness of death
Then the earth parted, and in pain I was pulled   110
From the world's womb, born again to the brightness
Of light. God's disciples dug me up,
Heaved me heavenwards, raised me and dressed me
In raiment of silver, garments of gold.

63

So now you know why, my friend in faith,   115
Though bitterly abandoned I was to sharp
Sorrow, now by all Creation's wondering
Creatures I'm widely worshipped:
Men in multitudes pray to my power,
Beseech this sign. On me God's bairn   120
In the pride of His Passion, knew on the cross
Punishment's pain: hence I'm now raised in glory
High under heaven, and him can I heal
Who my force fears. Once I was known
As the tree of torture, a sign of injustice;   125
Till I set all men on the road to righteousness.
See how through suffering I became highly favoured
By the world's Ruler, above all the wood's trees;
Just as Mary, God's mother,
Found grace and great favour   130
In the world, among women.
Now in love I invite you your dream to disclose,
Reveal your vision to the world in words.
Show all creatures the cross on which Christ redeemed
Mankind's many sins, and forgave Adam's fault.   135
It was he, our grand parent, who first death tasted;
But the Almighty ascended, the Redeemer arose
To heal that hurt. He died; He is risen;
And He will return, at the day of doom,
The Almighty Lord, with all his angels,   140
To seek out mankind on this middle-earth
And deliver His judgement. With the power
Of justice to all people He'll deal
Their just deserts, as each has deserved
In this little life. There's no-one so foolish   145
As to feel no fear when the Lord
Speaks His sentence. From that great crowd
Of the quick and the dead, He'll single out each,
And ask him to say, in God's honest truth,
If it's death he desires, the pangs of perishing,   150
Punishment's pain, as he Himself felt it
When fastened to the cross. Then they'll be
Tongue-tied, not know what to say
To the crucified Christ. But no-one who bears,
Bright in his breast this best of all signs   155
Need feel any fear. Far from earth's confines,
Through the might of the cross, that man will find heaven,
And live with the Lord.'

And so it befell
That alone, unbefriended, yet happy in heart
I acknowledged the cross. My spirit was stirred   160
To adventure a voyage, to fearlessly seek out
What fate holds in store. The height of my happiness
Is that this cross, before all appeals,
Accepts my prayers; so my hope of protection
Rests in that rood. I've no powerful companions   165
Alive on this earth to shield me from harm;
Hence they've departed to seek out the King,
To sojourn in glory with God Almighty
High in the heavens. Daily I long
For the day when that cross, clearly revealed   170
To me in a dream, will fetch me forth
From this empty existence, and in paradise place me
With the people of God in perpetual bliss,
Where I will find entire fulfilment
And endless joy. He who here among men   175
Suffered for our faults, gave Himself on the gallows
For our souls' sake, I know as my friend.
Such hope was restored
Of blessing and bliss, and many a poor soul
From death delivered, spared   180
From the pains of Hell's punishment,
When the Son in splendour, peerless in power,
Harrowed all Hell, and from darkness to light
Released innocent souls joyfully to join
The angelic host. Then that choice company,   185
Partners in praise, all raised one voice:
Sang Holy! and Holy! as the Highest came.
Absorbed in adoration, all angels rejoice
At the Hero's return to His heavenly home.

We have observed that the Anglo-Saxon poem familiarly known as *The Dream of the Rood* or *The Vision of the Cross* (it has no title in its manuscript form) occurs in the Vercelli Book, and therefore dates from the second half of the tenth century.[1] But the poem itself may be considerably older, perhaps seventh-century. Unusually for Anglo-Saxon poetry, there is relatively definite circumstantial evidence bearing upon this poem's date of composition and cultural location, since short extracts from a version of the same poem, or of an older poem from which both examples ultimately derive, is to be found inscribed in

Northumbrian runes on the Ruthwell Cross, a carved stone monument formerly housed in the church of Ruthwell in Dumfriesshire. The cross could be as old as AD 670.[2] Additionally some close verbal parallels occur in a short inscription on the 'Brussels Cross', a silver-laminated wooden crucifix (probably considered a fragment of the True Cross) which dates from the late tenth or eleventh centuries.[3] These could derive from the poem, or again from a common source.

We know the poem from a written source found within the sophisticated literary and intellectual context of late West-Saxon Christian culture, the culture of an already relatively united 'England'. But since we know that the historical substance of the poem was shared (at least) between an eighteen-foot stone monument, a fourteen centimetre silver-laminated wooden icon, and a literary document, we have to recognize that it was something larger than a poem: that the 'cross' constructed in the poem was a general cultural reality, a cross to be prayed to, and kissed, as well as a cross to be read.

Despite its acknowledged poetic unity – Richard Hamer aptly calls it 'the finest, most imaginatively conceived and most original of the Old English religious poems'[4] – the poem is in some ways a hybrid synthesis of diverse cultural, religious, and poetic discourses. Its formal organization echoes most of the different kinds of Anglo-Saxon poetry: the heroic (such as *Beowulf*), the biblical paraphrase (*Christ, Judith*), the saint's life (*Elene*), the elegy (*The Wanderer, The Seafarer*), the riddle (*Swordrack, Beam*), and the specimens of so-called 'gnomic' poetry.

The *Dream* is famous for its deployment of the language and imagery of heroic poetry, its sharing of a heroic vocabulary with poems like *Beowulf*, to dramatize the Passion of Christ. It contains a narrative which for some distance follows that of the Gospels, but then traces the subsequent life of the Dreamer, as does its companion-piece in the Vercelli Book, *Elene* (the story of the Emperor Constantine and his mother Helena, legendary discoverer of the True Cross). In its postulation of human existence as a *laene life*, a life both transitory and borrowed,[5] lying between a bright lost past and a radiant anticipated future, the poem shares the spiritual landscape of elegies such as *The Seafarer*. Where, in a passage of exhortation, the Cross dwells on the practical lessons implied by its revelation, we find moral advice of the kind typical of gnomic poetry. The stylistic personification of the Cross as speaking subject (*prosopopeia*) links it to the riddles, at least two of which have the Cross as their partial solution.[6]

In these respects the *Dream* is absolutely of and for its time, its formal devices deeply embedded in the linguistic registers and cultural vocabularies deployed by Anglo-Saxon poets across a wide range of poetic subjects and styles. Its obvious link with the Ruthwell Cross takes its history back deep into the very earliest stages of English society, to a point not long after the advent of Christianity (597 AD). Its medium of alliterative verse sets it within a cultural process by means of which a Germanic tradition of oral verse was assimilated to the norms of a monastic literacy originating in the Mediterranean.

The multicultural character of the literature produced from such a *rapprochement* of traditions is self-evident. It is quite another matter, on the other hand, to analyse within the literature the precise relations between those diverse cultural elements, since the record is already irreversibly translated into a European literacy that entered England only with the advent of Christianity. All the Anglo-Saxon poetry we have was documented, if not actually produced, in the environment of a Christian culture, as we have already seen from the example of Bede's account of Caedmon. There Bede shows both the English language and the Germanic verse-forms deployed obediently in the service of the Christian faith. Once Old English verse showed itself capable, in other words, of revealing through inspiration the word of God, it became worth noting and writing down (though not, admittedly, by Bede himself). The pagan traditions from which such poetry originated were, on the other hand, better discarded, and their verse with them: after all, as Bishop Alcuin put it, 'What has Ingeld to do with Christ? The eternal king reigns in Heaven, the lost pagan laments in Hell.'[7]

The relationships between Christian and pre-Christian traditions, literacy and orality, Mediterranean Christianity and Germanic paganism, lie at the heart of the *Dream*, and have been central to the history of its critical interpretation. The poem imagines the Crucifixion as a heroic combat, depicting Jesus as a *geong Haeleð*[8] ('young hero'), who approaches the challenge of the Passion like an epic hero girding himself for mortal combat:

'It was then that I saw a splendid Saviour
Approach with alacrity and courage to climb.
Hastily, the young hero stripped Him
For action...'

(ll. 43–6)

The indignity of the stripping of Christ's raiment in the Passion narrative is transformed, in the poem, into an eager and athletic stripping for battle. Here the Crucifixion is no humiliating subjugation: Jesus willingly embraces the Cross in a trial of strength and courage:

'In the sight of spectators,
Fearless and firm, keen for the combat,
He clambered on the cross.'

(ll. 47–9)

In the vocabulary of the Germanic heroic tradition, Christ is depicted not as a sacrificial lamb led to the slaughter, but as a fighter actively grappling an opponent:

'With shocks I shuddered, when the warrior wound
His strong arms about me...'

(ll. 59–60)

In death he lies as the finally defeated hero, subjugated yet magnificent in the scale of his epic achievement, and bitterly mourned by his surviving retainers:

'They took Him up
Tenderly, torn from His torture,
Left me blood-boltered, impaled by the points
Of annihilating nails. They stretched out His limbs,
Wounded, war-weary; stood at His head
To say their good-byes; grieved at his going,
They laid the exhausted hero to rest.'

(ll. 86–92)

In this way the poem reconstitutes the Passion-narrative into a form quite different from that encountered in the Gospels. Where the latter tend to distinguish the suffering victim from the triumphant risen God by narrative sequencing, the *Dream* by its use of heroic language brings into the Passion a dimension of epic heroism in action: reckless self-sacrificing bravery, and a triumph of heroic values even more poignant in defeat than in victory (although of course in this case, the victory of the Resurrection is implicit and yet to come). This certainly looks, *prima facie*, like cultural assimilation. As Bruce Mitchell puts it, 'the concept of Christ as a warrior-king'[9]

> must have appealed to a people who put such value on ferocious courage and pride and who lived according to the *comitatus* code in which the lord was the ring-giver and great hero for whom his warriors were duty-bound to die loyally and without complaint.

As these examples demonstrate, the presence within the poem of a Germanic warrior-ethic and a language of heroic values is in itself unproblematic. As one critic puts it, the poem fuses[10]

> words and ideas which stem from the Anglo-Saxon world rather than from the world of the Bible. In the *Dream of the Rood*, these two traditions are brought together. Christ is portrayed as the young hero, reigning from the Cross; but, at the same time, he is described as cruelly stretched out, weary of limb, enduring severe torment.

J. C. Pope reminds us, however, that these traditions can be 'brought together' in quite different ways:[11] 'Old English poetry shows at times the collision, but often the harmonious fusion, of Christianity and a submerged paganism, Mediterranean civilization and a more primitive but not always inferior Germanic world.' In what way are these two traditions poetically 'brought together' in the *Dream*, when they are so obviously and in so many respects entirely incompatible? Is it fusion or collision? It is one thing to draw parallels from narratives, archetypes, and symbols in different belief-systems; it is quite another to reconcile them. Certainly the figure of the heroic warrior can readily express certain types of divine power. The key role of the Anglo-Saxon lord or king as dispenser of gifts in return for loyalty and service could easily be assimilated to the Christian doctrine of grace. Even the death of a pagan hero or king in battle, and his memorialization in ritual, song, and poetry, could be seen as parallel to the death and resurrection of Christ.

But there the resemblances end. The combat undertakeh by Jesus has objectives quite different from those of an Anglo-Saxon raid or battle. It is not undertaken with a view to achieving political power or securing wealth through spoil or tribute. It is not a fight to settle a score or fulfil a vow of vengeance. Victory cannot be rendered visible by the defeat and subjugation of enemies; nor can the lord's authority be established by generosity in material rewards. Though Jesus may display Himself to onlookers as courageous (*modig on manigra gesyhðe*), the success he aims at has a goal more ambitious than the protection of a community or the defence of a kingdom: nothing less, indeed, than the universal Redemption of all mankind: *Þa he wolde mancyn lysan.*[12]

In short, this deployment of the Teutonic tradition as a formal vehicle for a narrative of the Christian Passion tends if anything to polarize rather than synthesize the alternative cultural perspectives. This is nowhere more apparent than in the mental torment of the Cross itself, which stoically bears physical punishment in sympathy with its Lord, but endures a sharper pang in the psychological double-bind of incompatible ethical imperatives. As has been correctly argued, the Cross sees itself to some degree as a loyal retainer in the *comitatus* of Christ. As such its duty is to defend its lord, to struggle against its lord's enemies, and if necessary to die protecting him. As one imbued with that heroic ethic, and bound by this high chivalric concept of nobility in service, the painful destiny of the Cross is to witness in enforced helplessness its lord's voluntary subjugation.

> 'Though all earth faltered
> And flinched with fear, I didn't dare
> To bend or to break. I'd have fallen full-length,
> Flat to the earth, but was forced to stand firm.
> I could have crushed each of those enemies,
> But by Christ's command I had to stand fast.'

(ll. 53–8)

Certainly at this point the heroic and triumphalist Christianity that doubtless appealed to pagan Anglo-Saxons happy to give their loyalty to an even greater, more glorious and more generous sovereign, co-exists uneasily with the Pauline doctrine of redemption through suffering, triumph through passivity.

The heroic language obviously derived from a world-view that was, despite its apparent religious dimensions, far more secular and materialistic, far less spiritual and otherworldly, than

Christianity. It is that essentially worldly cultural perspective that aligns Christ with the noble warrior whose being would naturally inhabit a social world of communal pleasures, 'hall-joys', ceremonies of ring- and gold-giving, childlike enjoyment of bright metals and precious stones – the world so vividly represented in terms of its loss in the heroic and elegiac poetry. The body in the Germanic tradition, as represented in the poems, is a real body that enjoys pleasure, suffers pain, and is subject to death. In so far as the Christ of the *Dream* is represented within that tradition, the poem is stressing the human and incarnational torment, rather than the abstract theological triumph, of the Crucifixion.

But the mortal and material body, of course, in Christian terms, reaches its end with death:

> *Hraew colode:*
> *faeger feorgbold*[13]
>
> [The corpse cooled:
> The beautiful life-container]

In *The Dream of the Rood*, the Cross's narrative leaves Christ at this point, a point which in human terms can only be conceived of and named as death. The beautiful body (*faeger hraew*) that proves to have been merely a dwelling-place for the spirit (*feorgbold*) lies empty and abandoned, chilling in ordinary mortal corruption (*colode*). The poem contains no empty tomb, no reassuring angelic visitors, no risen Lord. Christ is certainly imagined, at the end of the poem, appearing in full divine glory to harrow Hell. But that reference is a 'flashback' within the closing narrative of the dreamer, separated in time and space from the death on the Cross, a past example informing his own sure and certain hope for the future. In the central narrative of the Cross, which pursues the essential story of the gospels, we are left with nothing more encouraging than a dead body.

There is however, within the poem, a resurrection: it simply is not that of the risen Christ:

> 'For a second time
> They savagely felled me, ripped up my roots,
> Cruelly cast me in a deep pit.
> Earth closed coldly over my eyes, eyes
> That had seen God's dying. Days,

Years passed: and I perceived only
Comfortless clay, and the darkness of death.
Then the earth parted, and in pain I was pulled
From the world's womb, born again to the brightness
Of light. God's disciples dug me up,
Heaved me heavenwards, raised me and dressed me
In raiment of silver, garments of gold.'

(ll. 105–16)

It is the Cross, not the Christ, that experiences deposition, burial, exhumation, resurrection, and even ascension into divine glory.

The being of Christ in the *Dream* is represented, in my view, as the body of Germanic tradition: a strong and beautiful body, which fights bravely and conquers its enemies, but dies in the struggle, and is depicted finally as a dead hero, lying on the deserted battle-field, keenly cherished and bitterly mourned by those who owed its occupant their love and loyalty. The Resurrection of the poem is not of that body, but of the Cross, a sign (*beacen*) of the Passion and Redemption. As such it can be possessed as a material object, and revered for its organic symbolizing of the mystery in which it participated. It can be decorated with the gold, silver, and precious gems that were so beloved of Anglo-Saxon culture, and which so richly decorate the poetry as well as the artistry of the period. But above all it can function in the form either of material object of veneration or of abstract sign, as a ritual profession of faith, a liturgical focus of devotion, or a potent accessory to prayer.

At the same time, the poem doesn't simply substitute a symbolic Cross for a literal resurrection, exchange a lifted sign for a risen Christ. The Cross of the poem is represented not as an abstract symbol, but as a living being within whose nature both the agony and the mystery of the Passion are internalized. The sharing of Christ's agony by the anthropomorphized Cross is emphasized not in order that it might carry a burden of theological anxiety, but so as to render the agony of the Crucifixion present to the imagination, realized in sensory terms, and on a partially human scale. In his 'Vision of the Cross', the Dreamer sees not a fixed and abstract symbol, but a 'lively' and iterable sign, capable of signifying simultaneously agony and triumph:

Still through the gold my eyes descried
An ancient injury, the world's first wound,
Purple on gold, the passion and the glory,
As blood broke forth from the rood's right side.
Pierced with pity, and filled with fear
I was, as I saw that shifting sign
Alter its appearance, its colour change:
Now it was wet with the sweat of agony,
Now with brilliance of treasure bedecked.

(ll. 22–30)

What the Dreamer is looking at here is Christ Himself, incarnated in the pain and majesty of the Cross: always mortally wounded, always ascending into glory. The Cross has acquired those qualities by its sympathy in suffering, its proximity to the Passion: physically soaked in tangible sweat and blood, literally damaged by the violence of victimization. Hence the poem's imagining of the Cross as a variable and living sign is informed, via the legend of the True Cross and its discovery, by that vivid sensuous apprehension of its original ordeal.

By virtue of its participation in the Passion the Cross acquires a potent capability not only of expressing its mystery, but of facilitating the ritual memorialization, and more importantly, the imaginative re-enactment, of the Crucifixion itself. The kind of contemplation represented in the poem's dream-vision is essentially a form of 'spiritual exercise' in the method later formulated by St Ignatius:[14] an imaginative reconstruction, in the space between the meditating mind and ritual images, of a revealed theological truth.

It is at this point that the poem transcends its naturalistic and pagan inheritance. For here material things – gold, silver, jewels, even the body itself – become implements of devotional exercise and spiritual concentration rather than objects of value in themselves. The gold and jewels formerly distributed by the generous Anglo-Saxon lord have attained a new signifying potentiality as elements of a devotional icon. In that poignant description of the dead hero, the poem bids a sad but resigned farewell to its pagan ancestry.

Ultimately the poem is a meditation on, and an example of, the spiritual value of devotional art. A cross that speaks can exist

only in the poetry that speaks it. The Cross that exhorts the
Dreamer to put its self-revelation into words, does so in the
words of the poem that have already made such an exhortation
possible. And while the *Dream* internalizes this spiritual aesthetic
into a highly sophisticated literary form, it is the Ruthwell Cross –
a 'preaching Cross' that bears its evangelical speech inscribed
upon itself – that exemplifies in its totality the multicultural (and
'multi-media') character of this sacred art. In such great stone
memorials (as many as 1500 of which still survive) Anglo-Saxon
Christians could directly apprehend, in word and image, the
mystery of the Passion, and imaginatively recreate in their own
lives the suffering and triumph of their Saviour.

THE FALL OF THE ANGELS (338–441)

For Bryan Loughrey

Then he announced himself, that arrogant
Angel – formerly fairest of all heaven's
Host; brightest, most beautiful, beloved
Of his Lord, dear to the deity – until he turned
To the paths of pride, and the Highest Himself   5
Conceived a great anger against His angel,
Hurled him from heaven into punishment's
Pit, locked him from light into death's
Dark domain. Then the Ruler decreed
He should take a new name: this palace of pain   10
Inherit as home; be known as Satan,
Of darkness prince; and never against God
Raise angry arm.

So this same Satan, first among fiends,
Now reigns in Hell, who hitherto had served   15
In heaven the most High; the fairest of followers,
Till perverted by pride, he could no longer loyally
Yield to God's yoke. All's ill about his heart.
Pride pricks his breast, searing his soul,
Sensation more sore than the flames that afflict him.   20
In speeches of sorrow, in words of woe,
Satan in sadness spoke:
                  'How unlike this place,
This desolate domain, to the favoured world
From whence we fell: that land we have lost,   25

74

In high heaven's kingdom, God's great gift to me,
An angel's estate! Not that we knew
An occupant's pleasure, the pride of possession,
For more than a moment. He did us wrong
Who from heaven evicted, and hurled into exile   30
We who opposed Him, and threw us headlong
Into hottest Hell. Not enough He bereft us
Of our beautiful realm, robbed us of birth-right!
To another race of new-found favourites
Our land he enfiefed, planted our property   35
With his new-made man. That's my greatest grievance,
My principal pain. This unheard-of Adam,
A man made of mould, a son of the soil,
Should he sit in my seat, command in my kingdom,
Enjoy unearned glory, while I grieve in Hell?   40
If I were lent liberty to unharness my hands,
And escape from this prison for only one hour,
For the shortest shadow of a winter's day,
I could lead these legions ...
But I'm baffled, bound in with strong iron bonds,   45
Firmly I'm fettered with chafing chains.

'My force is enfeebled, that once was so strong:
Once potent, now powerless, weak as a child.
In the bonds of its burning, Hell holds me hard.
Above, below, underfoot, overhead,   50
Fire infernal fills this vast void.
No landscape was ever so wholly divested
Of charm and of comfort, no continent so
Cheerless: sulphurous burning, keen
Conflagration, ceaseless combustion, infinite   55
Flame. Here I'm locked in with links
Of a cast-iron chain, pinioned, paralysed,
Racked and restrained. My hands are hampered,
Fettered my feet. And could I burst free,
That heavy hell-door would obstruct my passage,   60
Forbid my flight. Bars of iron beset me:
Forge-founded fetters are fencing me in.
In prison I'm pent, and by the throat throttled.
I'm in God's grip.

                'I know he had knowledge   65
Of my mind's mysteries, I know that he knew
The secrets of our hearts. Mind-forged are these
Manacles, wrought for revenge. So now He who knows

Of all evil and enmity, knows conflict must come
Between Adam and me; that if I attacked him,   70
And fought with free hands, for his taking my
Territory, I'd bruise his heel.

     'Plainly we're put
To the torment of torture, here in this baleful, bottomless
Hell: and it's God who's engulfed us, swept us aside   75
Into this foul fog. Although it's apparent
He can pin nothing on us, allege no offence,
Convict of no crime, yet we're severed from sunshine,
Divided from daylight, of brightness bereft.
That conquering King has pitched us into   80
Perpetual pain. Nor can we hope
To wreak some revenge, or conveniently quit Him
For the loss of our light.

     'Now He's designed
A new domain for his parvenu playmate,   85
This toy that He's tinkered with, made
In his image. It's from Adam He hopes
To populate heaven with servile subjects,
With sinless souls. Let's carefully consider
If we upon Adam, and upon his offspring,   90
May visit some violence, work some wrong;
Some ingenious scheme to inhibit his hopes,
And dash his desires.

'I have no hopes of regaining that brightness,
To live in the light He thinks to possess   95
In perpetuity with His angel-powers. I don't aspire
To assault the Almighty, win over His weakness
Or subdue his strength. But what we dare do
Is to plunder that prize, that heavenly kingdom,
From its proud inheritor before he possess it.   100
If we can't keep it, neither can he.

'But better, let's bid him betray his maker,
Move him to mutiny against God's will;
Abandon his allegiance, forswear his fealty,
Deliver defiance to His kingly command.   105
Then the Lord will come down on them, God in His anger,
On their heads He'll rain the fire of His wrath:
Dismissed from His service, stripped of protection,
They'll be flung into exile, far from God's grace.
But here in Hell we'll welcome those wanderers,   110

And invite them to share our empire of shades.

       'With the best of your brains now,
Address this issue. It will strengthen our cause
To recruit as retainers those comradely creatures,
So the rest of their race may in iron indentures   115
Be sealed to our service. All you who in past years
I've richly rewarded, requited your service
With generous gifts: if ever there'll be
A convenient time to render repayment
That moment's arrived. Now's the time, noble thanes,   120
To thrust yourselves forward; to fettle your feathers
For adventurous flight; to climb through the clouds
And ascend the air. Now fling yourselves freely,
Vigorous in valour, across that great gulf;
Hover in the heavens, scale the blue skies,   125
By strength and by skill pass through Hell's portal
And penetrate paradise. There furtively find
Our earth-fashioned enemies, in their happy homeland,
Decked with delights: and drag them down swiftly
Into these dark dales.   130

       'There they stand, the Lord's
Loved ones, dear and desired,
Grasping the goods we should properly possess,
Reaping riches rightfully ours.
That's the favourable future marked out for mankind.   135
Oh, how that hurts me! How that maddens my mind!
Heavy in my heart is the thought that those creatures
Will inherit the earth, and all the world's wealth
Enjoy for ever. If any of you
Can seduce these His servants, tempt them to   140
Treachery, entice to betrayal
And breaking of faith, shortly you'll see
Fondness grow furious, love turn to hate.
If they let slip his loyalty, He'll be angry against them:
Their prospects will pale, their future recede   145
To a victim's vista of awful affliction,
A prisoner's vision of permanent pain.

       'Now apply your intelligence
To crack this conundrum: how may we seduce
God's sovereign son? On this rack of pain   150
I'd rest in peace, blissfully slumber,
Sleep soft in my bed, if my dear successor

I could see dispossessed.

'He who accomplishes this audacious adventure
Will win great reward from his grateful prince: 155
Titles and treasures in absolute possession
Will be wholly his. He who re-enters
This raging realm, flies back to these flames
To return the message of mankind's fall;
Who tells us that they, our wretchedest rivals,   160
Have forsworn their Father's foremost
Commandment, broken their maker's unbreakable
Bond, and sinned against God
In thought, word and deed:
He'll sit here beside me, that heaven-bound hero,   165
Potent and proud, here at my right
Hand. Even in these flames
We'll hereafter have
The firm satisfaction of fulfilled revenge.'

If poems like *Beowulf* and *The Battle of Maldon* contain pagan heroic materials which to one degree or another are Christianized, the extract translated above as *The Fall of the Angels* shows explicitly Judaeo-Christian materials assimilated to the Germanic heroic tradition. *The Fall of the Angels* is part of a long poem based on the Biblical Genesis, which covers the Old Testament narrative from the Creation of the world and of man, through the story of the Fall and the legendary foundations of the people of Israel. The Old English verse *Genesis* gives an account of the war in heaven following the rebellion of the archangel Lucifer. This sequence, like many other passages in the poem, cannot be found in the Biblical Genesis. Stories like the war in heaven, and the casting of Satan into Hell, his subsequent release and the subsequent seduction and Fall of mankind, are derived more directly from work of scriptural exegesis and interpretation written by the early Church Fathers (such as St Augustine's *City of God*) than from the biblical narratives proper. For instance, if you read the biblical account of the Temptation and Fall of man in *Genesis*, the serpent is not explicitly identified there as the Devil. The early Church Fathers pieced together various allusions within the biblical narratives and produced the continuous and consistent story of the rebellion of Lucifer, the Fall of the Angels, and the subsequent Fall of man which is very familiar to us from Milton's *Paradise Lost*.

In the middle of the Anglo-Saxon *Genesis* there appears the section from which the above extract is taken, and which, early scholars observed, repeats some of the poem's previous material. It was suspected by the scholar Sievers that an additional passage derived from an Old Saxon (that is, German) poem on the same subject had been interpolated into the manuscript. Sievers was fortunate enough to have his hypothesis confirmed when a fragment of exactly such an Old Saxon poem on the Fall of the Angels was discovered in the Vatican Library some eighteen years later. The poem given above is therefore at the very least a modern translation of an Anglo-Saxon version of an Old Saxon versification of Latin patristic works, which adapted and in many ways elaborated the Hebrew scriptures (and these in turn had already been translated into Greek and several other languages).

The section derived from the Old Saxon is now known as *Genesis B*, a poem of separate authorship contained within the larger framework of *Genesis A*. The poem sets out, just as Milton did in *Paradise Lost*, to narrate the events causing the great primal calamity of the Fall of man, and to dramatize its chief agent, the Devil. In undertaking that dramatization, the poet, again like Milton, found many aspects of Satan's character and career sympathetic and appealing rather than loathsome and contemptuous. The Satan of *Genesis B* is naturally constructed within the Germanic heroic tradition. He is a warrior who has fought bravely against a stronger opponent, and lost the battle. Cast down from his high position in heaven, deprived of all the status and privilege, as well as the manifest benefits of God's favour, and yet determined not to accept defeat, the Anglo-Saxon Satan reminds us irresistibly of Milton's fallen angel:

> What though the field be lost?
> All is not lost, th'unconquerable will,
> And study of revenge, immortal hate,
> And courage never to submit or yield...[15]

On the other hand, in expressing a poignant regret for the lost joys of heaven, Satan approximates very closely to the narrators of the elegiac 'exile' poems such as *The Wanderer* and *The Seafarer*. We are not told, in those poems, why the narrator is a dispossessed exile, a situation which could be attributed as plausibly to some crime as to an involuntary loss of protection and community. In other words, the situation of exile, and the powerful emotions of regret and despair associated with it, seems in some ways to have gripped the Anglo-Saxon poetic imagination more strongly than the specific legal or moral causes precipitating the exile in the first place.

To some extent Satan is certainly presented as culpable, in that he is guilty of disloyalty, a breach of trust and faith, a rejection of the loyalty demanded by his lord's otherwise unconditionally generous patronage. Such a breach of faith, together with the ingratitude it entailed, was certainly regarded as a particularly shameful form of treachery and betrayal. On the other hand there is considerably more ambiguity around the identification of Satan's particular offence, pride. An appropriate pride in one's ancestry, status, wealth, or personal achievement was a key ethical principle of Anglo-Saxon culture. A warrior was expected to boast of his achievements, both before a battle in order to intimidate the enemy, and to delight an audience after the event. There is no hint of criticism, for example, in the descriptions of Beowulf boasting of his heroic exploits and feats of superhuman strength.[16] We have also seen how, in *The Battle of Maldon*, a pride which can be overtly described as 'excessive' is none the less fully integrated into a positive view of the warrior ethic.[17] A modern reader, or even a contemporary military strategist, would be likely to question whether the interests of Byrhtnoth's sovereign Ethelred were better served by his *ealdorman*'s unquenchable appetite for action than they would have been by a tactical avoidance of combat that might have kept the territorial defences intact. Although the poem identifies Byrhtnoth's pride as *ofermod*, there is no indication that the defeat is attributed to this characteristic, one that a modern reader would find it very difficult to interpret as anything other than imprudence. In fact the heroic ethic is precisely aligned with the duality of military victory and defeat: it is the treacherous flight of Godric that loses the battle for the East Saxons, not the over-confidence which provokes their leader to seek conflict in the first place. When the Anglo-Saxon listener or reader read or heard this portrayal of Satan as a figure of indomitable and unquenchable pride, regretting the inheritance he has lost by the humiliation of defeat, but expressing an inflexible will and the courage not to yield, his emotional responses can be easily imagined as ambivalent or divided. For this was a heroic figure of a kind still highly valued even by a Christianized society, yet whose principal enterprise is the seduction and corruption of the human race itself, the great disaster which brought in its wake all human unhappiness.

Satan is also presented as a figure dedicated to revenge, an ethical code utterly rejected by Christian teaching. But Christianity had by no means extirpated the violent pleasures of vindictiveness from its culture: the psychological compulsions and ethical imperatives of revenge still acted strongly on the Anglo-Saxon imagination. In this respect, again, a poetic dramatization of Satan as a traditional Germanic hero is likely to have elicited complex responses from a culturally transitional readership or audience. Those still attached to some degree to the old codes of loyalty, and still committed to revenge as a form of justice, would surely have afforded him some admiration. On the other hand, since that very audience, as part of the human race, formed the object of the devil's vindictiveness, Satan was clearly cast as *feond mancynnes*, the enemy of man, as well as God's foe. As such he might be afforded a grudging respect; but since in the old code the proper response to a threat of vengeance would be retaliation in the same kind, the Anglo-Saxon Christian would have been left in no doubt about the proper treatment for this implacable old enemy.

5

Love Poetry

THE WIFE'S LAMENT

The song of myself is a sad, sad song.

Only I know of the troubles I've seen,
The suffering, the sorrow, the heartache, the hurt –
And always the keenest of all my cares
Is an exile's endurance, the hunger for home.   5
Since becoming a woman I've known such woe:
Early and late, present and past – but never
So much, no, never so much,
Never so much as now. Since the dawn
When my dear lord, across the wide waves,   10
Took his departure, far from his friends,
Each daybreak brings back to me all the same
Sorrow: where is my loved one?
Where's my lord gone?

   When I first came here,   15
Alone and unwelcome, to live with my lover,
Hunting for happiness, forlorn of all friends,
Scheming in secret my kinsmen conspired
To cleave us asunder, my new-found family
Pulled us apart. They wanted the whole world   20
To widen between us, so we'd live in longing
With no hope in our hearts;

My man had commanded me
To keep to this country, to live in this land
Though my friends here were few.   25
That's the source of my sadness:
Though I'd found a fellow with the sweetest smile,
With a face of friendship, free of all care –
His heart hid harm. He'd murder in mind.

How vainly we vowed that nothing in life   30
Would put us asunder; we'd keep one another
Till death did us part! Now that's all in the past;
Our bond is broken, borne on the wind,
Tossed on the tideway, gone without trace.

And though he's so dear, that violent vendetta –   35
That death-dealing duel, the feud that he fights for –
Means misery for me. Now those cruel kinsmen
Confine me to dwell in a forest fastness,
Under an oak, in a dreary dug-out
Scraped from the soil. Ancient this earth-work: 40
As old as my tears. My hovel's hedged in
By high-rearing hills, fenced in by forests
Of tangling briars. Piercing as thorns
Is my heart's sharp pain; dim as the dales
Is my darkening mind.   45

It's here, down here, that I feel most fiercely
The pain of that parting from my loved lord.
I think of the lovers who lie in their beds,
Soundly asleep in each other's arms;
While I every daybreak, here in my hole,   50
Under my oak-tree, wake to awareness
Of the love I've lost. Here I must sit,
In a sadness of shade, through the tedious light
Of a long summer day. Here I must weep
A wanderer's woes, the tears of an exile.   55
I can never assuage the sighs of my soul,
Never bring peace to my hungering heart,
Never know rest from the longings of love;
Know no cessation of the breast's bitter cares.

But I'm sure my young man   60
Has anxieties too. A man has to carry
A carefree appearance, make out he's tough,
Though his heart may be broken, and weeping within.
There's no joy in the world save that we can win
From our own tormented hearts. For he, my dear lord,   65
He also is far, far away from his friends, far
From his homeland. I'm sure, as he sits,
Under some stone-cliff, frozen with frost,
Assaulted by storms, in some desolate homestead
Cut off by the tides, he too will be nursing   70
Pitiless hurt, he too will remember

A happier home. Are those who endure
Love's harsh longings
Always, forever, sad?

There has been very little reference in these pages to women.[1]
All the poems presented and discussed above, whether heroic,
elegiac, or devotional, seem to dwell on the experience of men:
men in battle, men suffering the anguish of exile, men
experiencing spiritual ecstasy. One would perhaps not expect
to hear much about women in the heroic literature, given that
they, together with children and animals, were objects to be
protected by masculine violence. Aristocratic women naturally
had an important role to play in Anglo-Saxon courts, and this is
reflected in various references to queens exercising the graces of
hospitality, as does Hrothgar's queen Wealhtheow in *Beowulf*.[2]
But the heroic poems (with a few notable exceptions) do not
generally contain portrayals of warrior women.

It would be equally natural to assume that the monastic and
Christian culture within which the poems were committed to
manuscript, and possibly composed, would inevitably have
been exclusively male. This, however, is not the case, since
women played a particularly central role in the early Christian
church (a role which, in some churches, they are still attempting
to recover). The religious community at Whitby, where
Caedmon received his inspiration, was 'co-educational': a
combined monastery and convent. The leader of the community at the time of this event was the formidable Abbess Hild.

We do not know whether there were any women poets, but
then we have virtually no idea of the identity or character of any
of the poets, with the exception of Caedmon, whose legend has
survived better than his poems. The only other named poet from
the period, Cynewulf, was presumably a man (of course, if we
knew no better, we would say the same of George Eliot).
Scandinavian literature contains many myths and legends about
female warriors like the Valkyries; however, they don't turn up
in the surviving corpus of Anglo-Saxon poetry. On the other
hand, the Christian poets were obviously impressed enough
with some legendary heroic women from the Old Testament,
and some celebrated female saints, to write poems like the short
epic *Judith* (found in the same manuscript as *Beowulf*), the
heroine of which is portrayed as a saint, and as a woman fully

capable of masculine courage and violence; and the saint's life *Elene*, which celebrates the determined and resourceful Helena, legendary finder of the True Cross, and mother of Constantine, the first Christian Emperor of Rome.

There are many examples of historical periods which have long appeared to be almost exclusively masculine preserves, and yet which have subsequently delivered to cultural analysts substantial evidence of women as writers, readers, producers, patrons, and facilitators (like Hild) of the literary arts. There seems to be no reason in principle why the Anglo-Saxon period should not in due course become another such example.

This chapter is entitled 'Love Poetry' despite the inevitably small selection of work upon which such a category is obliged to be based. There are really only three poems that may be assigned to such a category, poems that display the features of lyrical expression and emotional intensity we would expect to find in the poetry of love. My assumption is that these poems are the tip of the iceberg, and that the failure of Anglo-Saxon love poetry to survive on any large scale has more to do with the criteria of selection employed by Christian scribes than with any lack of interest in, or enthusiasm for, the subject. At the same time, it would be true to say that nothing like a pure love lyric, dealing purely and in isolation with romantic emotions, exists from this period. The poems that do survive deal with matters that are common to other kinds of poetry, as well as with individual relationships. Two of the poems are dramatic monologues, imagined as spoken by women. The third, which is not included here, known as *The Husband's Message*,[3] is a poem that has culturally been linked with *The Wife's Lament*, since it contains a message, carved in runes on a stick, from a lover or husband to the woman from whom he has been separated by a feud, telling her that he is rich and successful, and urging her to cross the seas to rejoin him. The poem is in some ways like a riddle, since the dramatic speaker is the anthropomorphized stick that carries the message. The man described in the poem certainly displays that cheerful demeanour the woman in *The Wife's Lament* seems to have found so misleading and deceptive:

> Me, I'm a man who's conquered all care:
> Nothing I need, no generous gift, no gold,
> No garden of earthly delights – provided,
> Princess, I could possess you.

85

Again it should be recalled that the titles are editorial accretions, designed to link the poems into a single connected narrative. They both appear in the Exeter Book, but not consecutively; and may well have nothing more to do with one another.

The Wife's Lament begins with a familiar expression of sadness and deprivation. We recognize immediately that we are dealing here with yet another exile, nostalgically regretting another lost past. The poem then immediately sounds a different note from *The Wanderer* and *The Seafarer*. In those poems of masculine exile, the cause of exile, though not necessarily explained, dates from some decisive event in the man's life – the Wanderer, for example, dates his exile from the burial of his dead lord. The woman in *The Wife's Lament*, however, sees exile as a more existential condition, and seems to relate it directly to her gender, to the beginning of female adulthood – *siððan ic up weox* ('since I grew up'). I have made the assumption that she is talking about growing up into a woman, rather than growing up generally, and I have for that reason strengthened the emphasis on gender, assuming that womanhood, rather than just maturity, is the root of her woe.

The poem then goes on to provide the woman's story within the dramatic monologue framework. Because of the elliptical nature of some of the expressions in the poem, critics have disagreed about the structure of this background narrative. The woman is evidently an *émigrée* who has married into another tribe. She loved her husband and had great hopes of the marriage. She seems, however, not to have been accepted by her husband's kin, who perhaps have regarded her, with some ethnic dislike, as a foreigner. The tribe seems to have been, or to have become, involved in some feud, and the husband has been chosen to perform some action, probably to kill someone, within it. In the poem the woman sees these events as a deliberate conspiracy to separate her husband from her. It is, we infer, as a consequence of this killing (or some other serious crime – *morthor*, here translated as 'murder', could mean either) that the husband has to go into exile, and the couple become separated.

The poem expresses with great poignancy and eloquence the combined emotions of separation from the one she loves and isolation within an unsympathetic community. Like the narrator in the elegiac poems, she remembers the pleasures of the past;

but whereas within the masculine discourse of those poems, the regretted past is defined as the social world of 'hall-joys', what she regrets is the pleasing and supportive presence of her lover. Compare, for instance, the passage from *The Wanderer* in which the exile remembers his relationship with his lord –

> The man who's lost the cheerful counsel
> And cherishing love of a charitable host,
> Harbours a hurt that hits him hard.
> When sleep and sorrow, subtly linked,
> Lull the loner in deception of dreams,
> His fantasy fills with voiceless visions
> Of the love he's lost. He kens that he kisses
> His loved liege-lord; with head and hands
> Caresses his knee; remembers the rites
> Of gift and service, the endless exchanges
> Of loyalty for love.

– to the woman's elegy for her broken marriage:

> It's here, down here, that I feel most fiercely
> The pain of that parting from my loved lord.
> I think of the lovers who lie in their beds,
> Soundly asleep in each other's arms;
> While I every daybreak, here in my hole,
> Under my oak-tree, wake to awareness
> Of the love I've lost.

The poem expresses the woman's suffering, her unhappiness and isolation in a very vivid way. In addition, it seems to me that a specifically feminine character comes through the poem in the woman's expressions of bitterness and resentment against the masculine activity of vengeance and violence which takes her husband away from her.

> And though he's so dear, that violent vendetta –
> That death-dealing duel, the feud that he fights for –
> Means misery for me.

Though there must, she speculates, be advantage to someone in this conflict, it provides no conceivable benefit to her. She is badly treated by her husband's kin, being required to live outside the community in some kind of cave or primitive shelter, which becomes a metaphor for her powerful sense of abandonment and isolation. She is doubly punished for her love, first by separation from her lover, and second by exile from the community from which he has been obliged to flee. Images drawn from a natural landscape of dark moors, enclosing forests, tangling briars, locate her at the centre of a topography comparable to the enchanted landscape of the folk-tale *Sleeping Beauty*.

The poem then shifts remarkably to a focus on the parallel isolation and unhappiness of her exiled lover. She is not so isolated within the world of her own suffering as to be unable to appreciate that he may be suffering too. The capacity of love to imagine empathetically the lover's situation facilitates a remarkable reflection on the pressures of masculinity. Not only, the female narrator says, does her lover endure a very similar heartache, for him it is exacerbated by the harsh pressures of a masculine code that precludes any such tenderness of 'womanly' feeling. His grief, she imagines, is compounded by his need to display a robust and unfeeling exterior. In this way the poem rises above self-pity to a general reflection on the way in which love, entangled with the complexities of social life, can bring more misery than happiness to both man and woman.

WULF AND EADWACER[4]

My folk must feel they've been given a gift.
If they face an attack, they'll take him by force:
And still we'll be sundered,
   Severed and separate,
     Painfully parted,
       As now.
Wulf is on one isle, I on another.
His island's secured, fenced in by fens.
Savage soldiers defend my shores.
If they face an attack, they'll take him by force:
And still we'll be sundered,
   Severed and separate,
     Painfully parted,
       As now.
I've wept for my Wulf
Interminable tears. Wrapped in a cold
Curtain of rain, when the warrior wound
His warm arms about me, the pang of my pleasure

88

Was pierced with pain. Pity my pining:
By affection, not food, I need to be nourished.
O Wulf, my Wulf, I'm ill at your absence:
Woeful with watching, weary with waiting,
Knowing you'll never come. Will my complaint reach
Eadwacer's ears? He'll see soon enough,
When a wolf to the woods
Rustles his wretched whelp.

How simple to sever
What never
Was one! How easy to jolt
Into jangling discord
The music we made together!

This poem is again a dramatic monologue imagined as spoken by
a woman; and once more it is about a love relationship rendered
complex and difficult by social pressures and obligations. As with
The Wife's Lament, the narrative context implied by the poem is
not easy to get at, and editors and translators normally have to
select a preferred explanation from a number of different options.
My translation assumes that the woman and her lover, or
husband, Wulf, are separated from one another and confined on
two islands by the exigencies of a feud. The woman functions
almost as a hostage, since her people expect Wulf to attempt to
reach or rescue her (this is one of the possible meanings of the
term *lac*, gift). The woman has been befriended, or possibly even
married, by a member of her own clan whom she accepts, and to
whose embraces she to some degree responds. She continues,
however, to pine for Wulf, who clearly remains her true and
original lover. There appears to be a child, possibly not yet born,
though the syntax doesn't indicate whether Wulf or Eadwacer is
the father. She expects Wulf to try to take the child, either to
recover his own son, or to steal or possibly even kill the son of
Eadwacer.

The ambiguities surrounding the narrative which we are
obliged to construct around the poem do not, however, detract
from its poetic power. Its real imaginative beauty consists in its
overt expression of powerful emotions: the anguish of separation; the mingled pain and pleasure of the new relationship; the
physical longing for the absence of a loved one. The image of the
two lovers imprisoned on two separate islands, kept from one

another by distance, by the barrier of water, by the savagery of organized military violence, and by the deep cultural divisions of inter-tribal conflict and feud, gives a particularly vivid insight into the Anglo-Saxon world from an unusual perspective, which in turn prefigures much later conceptions of humanity as isolated within an unfriendly universe.

The poem's metaphors in turn reveal a rich fertility of meanings. The gift (*lac*) which is mentioned in the first line could relate to the position of the woman herself as an internal hostage within her own tribe (she provides the bait which is calculated to bring Wulf within their hostile grasp). Or the word *lac* has been interpreted to refer to her pregnancy by Eadwacer, the gift of an as-yet unborn child, which seems to the tribe a piece of good fortune, but to her forebodes danger since she expects Wulf to attempt to steal or recover it. Possibly she knows the child to be Wulf's while Eadwacer thinks it his.

Similarly, the poem ends with an observation that could apply equally to the woman's relationship with either or both of her lovers. Two metaphors are in play, one that of separation or division, the other that of harmony or concord. The intimacy of a relationship is so easily broken; the harmony of a marriage so quickly thrown out of tune. But whether she is referring to her original relationship with Wulf, or to the marriage of convenience with Eadwacer, or indeed, ambiguously, to both, remains tantalizingly obscure.

Even at its most intimate and personal, then, Anglo-Saxon poetry remains concerned with some of the central preoccupations of the historical culture. Even these poems of love, which display an emotional plangency as moving and eloquent as can be found in any romantic verse, address the joys and sufferings of love within a context prescribed by the key social loyalties and betrayals of Anglo-Saxon England: by family conflicts and violence; by feud and exile; by the harsh privations of an inhospitable environment rendered all the more harsh when not gladdened and warmed by personal affection, social pride, and communal pleasure.

The other noteworthy characteristic of these poems is that, unlike all the other types of poetry examined in this study, they bear no trace of religious language, and exhibit no vestige of Christian belief. It is as if, while the powerful principle of loyalty to a lord could be transferred relatively easily to a Christian love of God, the love between man and woman was an altogether more embedded and intractable value, for the loss of which no spiritual emotion could ever fully compensate.

Conclusion

In order fully to grasp the depth and breadth, the vitality and sophistication of Anglo-Saxon culture, it is of course necessary to go beyond the poetry, and to read among the diversity of written records, in verse and prose, which cover such forms as historical and theological writing, moral and ethical treatises, political and geographical studies, legal records, and so on. An anthology such as Bradley's *Anglo-Saxon Poetry* provides a good sense of the diversity and quality of Anglo-Saxon poetry and prose.

To my mind it is with the poetry that one should begin, since everything of interest in Anglo-Saxon history is also to be found there: all the historical and political, moral and ethical, theological and ecclesiastical, military and constitutional motives and preoccupations of the culture can be read, in the verse, at the level of individual perception and personal experience. Here we can understand what it was like to be part of an Anglo-Saxon community, and how it felt to become lost to it; what it was like to be a Christian speaking and writing in a language that for centuries had expressed pagan values and beliefs; what it felt like to be a soldier in the tenth century, standing with all the splendour of the heroic past behind you, and a cruel and determined enemy in front; what it felt like to be a woman occupying a servile position in a male-dominated society, and how it was for a man putting on a brave face to hide a deep inward sorrow. Nothing but poetry can take us into a historical period with this degree of empathy, give us access to so inward and vivid a knowledge of human experience in such a culture and such a society.

The many parallels and details of comparison between Anglo-Saxon culture and our own should not, however, allow us to forget that this is a very foreign world, in which the past really was another country, where things were done differently. The particular moral and psychological conflicts represented in the poetry are not ours, since the values held by these our remote ancestors were not ours – though it is true that the manner in which they struggled with those conflicts is often, no doubt, reminiscent of moral exploration in any age.

This paradox of sameness with difference, which is true historical knowledge, is somewhat distorted by translation, since in a translation the strangeness of the past has already been to some extent integrated and explained in terms intelligible to the present. All the more reason, then, to attempt at least some encounter with the foreign language itself, Anglo-Saxon English, in which that remote and alien past formulated its experience. The foreignness of the language should prevent any too easy assumption of familiarity, any unmediated reference from present to past.

As an impetus towards further study I have provided here a section of *The Dream of the Rood*, in the original Old English, from Swanson's edition, together with a literal line-by-line translation in order to make it possible to follow the original. Below is the same section from my own verse translation, with some notes and commentary indicating how the modern version inevitably interprets and adds to the original, even while striving to maintain fidelity to its unique, inimitable, and unrepeatable lost voice.

93

THE DREAM OF THE ROOD (ll. 33–49)

Geseah ic   þa Frean mancynnes
Saw I then   the Lord of mankind

eftsan elne mycle   þaet he me wolde on gestigan.
hasten with great courage   in order that he might me ascend.

Þaer ic þa ne dorste   ofer Dryhtnes word
There I then not dared   against God's word

bugan oððe berstan   þa ic bifian geseah
bend or break   when I tremble saw

eorðan sceatas.   Ealle ic mihte
earth's surfaces.   All I might

feondas gefyllan   hwaeðre ic faste stod.
enemies fell   notwithstanding I stood fast.

Ongyrede hine þa geong haeleð,   (þaet waes God aelmihtig),
Prepared himself then the young hero,   (that was God Almighty),

strang ond stiðmod;   gestah he on gealgan heanne,
firm and resolute   mounted He on gallows high

modig on manigra gesyhðe,   þa he wolde mancyn lysan.
brave in the view of many,   when He would mankind redeem.

Bifode ic þa me se beorn ymbclypte;   ne dorste ic hwaeðre bugan to eorðan,
I trembled when the warrior embraced me;   nor durst I however bend to earth,

feallan to foldan sceatum.   Ac ic sceolde faeste standan.
fall to earth's surface.   For I had to firm stand.

Rod waes ic araered.   Ahof ic ricne Cyning,
As a cross I was raised.   Lifted I up the powerful King,

heofona Hlaford;   hyldan me ne dorste.
the Lord of heaven;   I dared not flinch.

Þurhdrifan hi me mid deorcan naeglum;   on me syndon þa dolg gesiene,
Pierced they me with dark nails;   on me are the wounds seen,

opene inwid-hlemmas.   Ne dorste ic hira naenigum sceððan.
the open wounds of malice.   Nor durst I any injure.

Bysmeredon hie unc butu aetgaedere.

Reviled they us both together.

begoten of þaes guman sidan,
sprung from the man's side

Eall ic waes mid blode bestemed,
All I was with blood soaked

siððan he haefde his gast onsended.
when he his spirit relinquished.

TRANSLATION (ll. 43–73)

It was then that I saw a splendid Saviour
Approach with alacrity and courage to climb.
Hastily, the young hero[1] stripped Him
For action, girded like a gladiator
Ready for the ring. In the sight of spectators,
Fearless and firm, keen for the combat,
He clambered on the cross. He sought no insignia
Of cruel conquest, no brows bound
With victorious wreaths:[2] His reward
Was mankind's Redemption,[3] salvation of souls
His only prize. Though all earth faltered
And flinched with fear, I didn't dare
To bend or to break. I'd have fallen full-length,
Flat to the earth, but was forced to stand firm.
I could have crushed each of those enemies,
But by Christ's command I had to stand fast.
With shocks I shuddered, when the warrior wound
His strong[4] arms about me: but I daren't stir.
More forbidding than fear was the Lord's Word.[5]
Crude and rough-hewn, a cross of wood I was:
Yet I lifted on high the Lord of Hosts;
I held aloft the might of majesty.[6] Black nails
Battered through me, opening wide
The wounds of wickedness.[7] When they scoffed[8]
At the Saviour, their spit spattered
Me. In His blood when it sprang
From His side, was my splintered surface
Soaked. In the thrust of a spear[9]
Was His spirit's expense, when all
Was accomplished, when life He relinquished,
And gave up the Ghost.[10]

95

Notes to the Translation

1 The key-word in this passage is *haeleð* ('hero'), which focuses the multicultural character of the poem, and informs its narrative of the crucifixion as an epic combat, entered with both spiritual zeal and physical courage. I've used the figure of the gladiator to suggest an eager acceptance of a formal combat, to the death, conducted in front of spectators: which in turn stresses the physical athleticism entailed in the poem's imagery of Jesus actively climbing onto the cross.

2 A familiar Shakespearean echo: from *Richard III*'s famous opening soliloquy, Act I, scene i.

3 I've elaborated the poem's reference to the Redemption by spelling out the implicit contrast between the spoils of battle available to a successful pagan warrior, and the victory attainable in this particular fight – *he wolde mancyn lysan* ('he wished to deliver/ redeem mankind').

4 Again, by the language of heroism the crucifixion is represented not as a subjection, but as an active intervention. To enhance that effect I've added 'strong' to the arms that voluntarily embraced (*ymbclypt*) the cross.

5 The poem intersperses narrative depiction of Christ's heroic actions with expressions of fear and self-reproach from the Cross. The effect is a powerful antiphonal dialectic I have found impossible to emulate, so the order of phrases is rearranged in the translation. I've assimilated the phrase *Dryhtnes word* ('God's command') to the New Testament's recuperation of the Old Testament law – 'In the beginning was the Word' (John 1: 1).

6 Since *rode* is both 'tree' and 'cross', these lines deliver a range of possible meanings, paraphrasable from the proud affirmation, 'I, the Cross, was erected to raise the powerful king,' to the wondering paradox, 'A mere piece of wood, I was raised to hold aloft the powerful king.' I have emphasized the latter possibility, attempting to disclose both the magnitude of the event, and the effort and achievement of the cross's own contribution.

7 Both *þurhdrifan* ('pierced') and *inwid-hlemmas* ('deep injuries') convey the same immediate physical sense of penetration, of deep internal wounding.

8 In order to create a precise sensory focus for *Besmyredon* ('mocked, reviled') I've merged the mockery of the chief priests (Matthew 27: 41), with earlier physical abuse from the soldiers: 'And they spit upon him...and smote him on the head' (Matthew 27: 30). See also Mark 25: 32: 'And they that were crucified with him reviled him'. In St Luke's gospel it is the soldiers and the thieves who perform the

mockery.

9 The spear-thrust occurs only in St John's Gospel: 'one of the soldiers with a spear pierced his side, and forthwith came there out blood and water' (19: 34). In *The Dream of the Rood*, as the cross is drenched in blood from the wound in Jesus's side, so it is redeemed: 'We have redemption through his blood...having made peace through the blood of his cross' (Colossians 1, 14: 20). The triple image-complex of blood, water, and spirit represented in St John's account is, of course, central to Christian theology and worship.

10 Both 'relinquished' and 'gave up the ghost' (Luke 23: 46) are justified by the phrase *he haefde his gast onsended* ('he had sent his spirit away') – not a submission to death, but an active and voluntary dismissal of life. My 'accomplished' is the New Testament's 'It is finished' (only in John 19: 30).

Notes

INTRODUCTION

1 Religious considerations also motivated early Anglo-Saxon studies during the Reformation. In their concern to revise Roman Catholic dogma, John Bale and John Foxe regarded Anglo-Saxon manuscripts as evidence of the English origins of Christianity; ancient scriptural writing in the vernacular supported their claim for biblical authority being generally accessible. Foxe complained that many Roman practices were 'new nothynges lately coyned in the minte of Rome without any stampe of antiquitie'. Similarly, in the reign of Elizabeth I, Archbishop Matthew Parker was encouraged to research the early English church, which permitted married clergy and queried transubstantiation, to justify the independence of the national church from the papacy. See Allen J. Frantzen, *Desire for Origins: New Language, Old English, and Teaching the Tradition* (New Brunswick and London: Rutgers University Press, 1990), 'Renaissance Anglo-Saxonism', pp. 35–45.

2 It is remarkable that Anglo-Saxon was rarely taught in universities before the twentieth century, except in the USA, where the University of Virginia had it in the curriculum and Thomas Jefferson wanted to introduce it in primary schools. See Frantzen, *Desire for Origins*, p. 15.

3 Consider the different position of modern speakers of ancient British languages such as Welsh and Gaelic.

CHAPTER 1. ANGLO-SAXON VERSE

1 Bede, *Ecclesiastical History of the English People*, trans. Leo Sherley-Price, revised R. E. Latham (Penguin, 1955, revised 1990), p. 248.

2 I am not suggesting that there never was a poet called Caedmon: only that the status of the story within Bede's narrative has more to

do with founding mythology and legend than with anything we would think of as accurately documented historical fact.

3 Copies of the *Lindisfarne Gospels* show the Latin text interlineated with a Northumbrian Old English gloss. See Henry Noel Humphries, *The Illuminated Books of the Middle Ages* (1849; London: Bracken Books, 1989), Pl. 1.

4 The first five books of the Old Testament were translated into Old English around 1000: *The Old English Heptateuch*, ed. S. J. Crawford (London: Early English Text Society, 1922).

5 The Latin paraphrase is provided in *Sweet's Anglo-Saxon Reader*, revised by C. T. Onions, 14th edition (Oxford: Clarendon Press, 1876, revised 1959), p. 166.

6 The West-Saxon version of the *Hymn* is printed in the course of an extract from the Old English translation of Bede, in *Sweet's Anglo-Saxon Reader*, p. 43. I have here converted the Old English poem into a hymn, compatible with a traditional hymn tune *Epiphany* (in the Anglican *New English Hymnal* (Norwich: Canterbury Press, 1986).

I

Now let us praise highest heaven's Protector,
Praise we the Lord for his purpose and power;
Praise we the works of the Father of Glory,
Maker of all from Creation's first hour.

II

Wonders He wrought at the dawn of Creation
Earth He established, the skies and the sea;
Gave us the heavens as a roof for our dwelling,
Maker of all things, Infinity.

III

Now let us praise all the works of the Father,
Mighty in power, perfect in mind;
God of eternity, only Creator,
Praise for the world He has made for mankind.

7 The Dutch scholar Junius in 1655 published a manuscript containing a collection of poems that resembles Bede's list of Caedmon's works, and attributing them to Caedmon. There is no other evidence to link the poems with the poet, and scholars believe them to have been the work of several authors.

8 Stephen Pollington, *An Introduction to the Old English Language and its Literature* (Frithgarth: Anglo-Saxon Books, 1994, revised 1996), pp. 10–11.

9 Ibid., p. 10.

10 *Sweet's Anglo-Saxon Reader* provides both the West-Saxon and the Northumbrian texts, pp. 43 and 166.

11 For an accessible linguistic introduction to Anglo-Saxon, see Helmut Gneuss, 'The Old English Language', in *The Cambridge Companion to Old English Literature*, eds. Malcolm Godden and Michael Lapidge (Cambridge: Cambridge University Press, 1991). It should also be noted that elsewhere in England, for example in the north-west, different dialect forms produced very different literature – such as *Sir Gawain and the Green Knight*, which has much in common with older alliterative verse.

12 Francis P. Magoun, Jr., 'The Oral-Formulaic Character of Anglo-Saxon Narrative Poetry', *Speculum*, 28 (1953), pp. 446–67; quoted from Lewis E. Nicholson (ed.), *An Anthology of 'Beowulf' Criticism* (Notre Dame, Ind.: Notre Dame University Press, 1963), p. 189.

13 *Beowulf*, ed. John Porter (Frithgarth: Anglo-Saxon Books, 1991), ll. 867–74. Porter's edition is useful in having a literal, facing-page, line-by-line translation.

14 We might, for example, have of *The Dream of the Rood* only the fragmentary version carved in Northumbrian runes on the Ruthwell Cross; see Ch. 4, and Michael Swanton's edition of the poem (Manchester: Manchester University Press, 1970; revised edition, Exeter: University of Exeter Press, 1987), pp. 9–38. It is interesting to speculate on whether the poems of the Gawain-poet represent a continuous survival of alliterative verse in oral tradition, or simply a literary revival of what was perceived as an antique metrical convention.

15 'Old English poetry is descended from a preliterary stock once common to the Germanic tribes of the European continent... Writing as a literary art...was introduced among the Anglo-Saxons in the course of the seventh century by missionaries from the Mediterranean world and from Ireland.' J. C. Pope, *Seven Old English Poems* (New York: Bobbs-Merrill, 1966; revised edition, New York: Norton, 1981), p. 43.

16 Cynewulf's *Elene* is translated into prose by S. A. J. Bradley in *Anglo-Saxon Poetry* (London: Dent, 1982), pp. 164–97.

17 The Old Icelandic sagas were written down in the twelfth and thirteenth centuries, e.g. by Snorri Sturleson. See for example his *Heimskringla: the Olaf Sagas 1–2*, trans. S. Laing, revised J. Simpson (London: 1964).

18 *Beowulf*, ed. Porter, l. 90.

19 *Beowulf*, ed. Porter, l. 1.

20 Of course, if we think of the poem as pre-Christian, then it can't have included an account of the Creation.

21 Genesis, ll. 6–25. This and other references to the *Holy Bible* relate to the *New Revised Standard Edition* (Cambridge: Cambridge University Press, 1989).

22 See e.g., F. P. Blackburn: 'It is admitted by all critics that *Beowulf* is essentially a heathen poem'. 'The Christian Coloring of the *Beowulf*', PMLA 12/2 (1897), pp. 205–25; quoted from Nicholson (ed.), *An Anthology of 'Beowulf' Criticism*, p. 1.

23 '*Beowulf*... can be approached as a reinvention of the legendary Germanic past by a poet who was about as distant from this age as living Americans are from Elizabethan England.' John D. Niles, 'Pagan Survivals and Popular Belief', in Godden and Lapidge (eds.), *The Cambridge Companion to Old English Literature*, p. 137.

24 For the co-existence of pagan and Christian values in Anglo-Saxon poetry see my 'From Exile to Pilgrim: Pagan and Christian Values in Anglo-Saxon Elegiac Verse', in *English Literature, Theology and the Curriculum*, ed. Liam Gearon (London: Cassell, 1999), pp. 63–84.

25 See 'The Electronic Beowulf', accessible through the British Library's website.

26 Prose translations of *Widsith and Waldere* appear in Bradley, *Anglo-Saxon Poetry*, pp. 336–40 and 510–12.

27 Most of these poems are translated into prose in R. K. Gordon, *Anglo-Saxon Poetry* (London: Dent, 1926, rev. 1954), and Bradley, *Anglo-Saxon Poetry*. Verse translations of *Genesis*, *Elene* and *Doomsday* appear in *Early English Christian Poetry*, trans. Charles W. Kennedy (London: Hollis and Carter, 1952).

28 Examples of these types can be found in *The Battle of Maldon and Other English Poems*, trans. Kevin Crossley-Holland, ed. Bruce Mitchell (London: Macmillan, 1965); and in Richard Hamer (ed.), *A Choice of Anglo-Saxon Verse* (London: Faber and Faber, 1979).

29 Michael Swanton (ed.), *The Dream of the Rood*.

30 Hamer (ed.), *A Choice of Anglo-Saxon Verse*, p. 163.

31 *The Earliest English Poems*, trans. Michael Alexander (Harmondsworth: Penguin, 1966), p. 30.

32 See Seamus Heaney's translation of *Beowulf* (London: Faber and Faber, 1999), especially his Introduction, p. xxiii.

CHAPTER 2. HEROIC POETRY

1 The standard scholarly edition of *Beowulf* is *Beowulf and the Fight at Finnsburg*, ed. Fr. Klaeber (3rd edition, Boston, 1950); the standard student editions are those of C. L. Wrenn, revised W. F. Bolton (London, 1973), and George Jack (Oxford, 1994). John Porter's edition (see Chapter 1, n. 13), includes a facing-page literal

translation.

2 Fred C. Robinson, 'Beowulf', in Godden and Lapidge (eds.), *The Cambridge Companion to Old English Literature*, p. 145.

3 *Beowulf*, ed. Porter, l. 1.

4 Ibid.

5 J. R. R. Tolkien, 'Beowulf: The Monsters and the Critics', *Proceedings of the British Academy*, 22 (1936), pp. 245–95; quoted from Nicholson (ed.) *An Anthology of 'Beowulf' Criticism*, p. 88.

6 *Beowulf*, ed. Porter, ll. 3137–82. In 1939 a burial ship, apparently the tomb of a seventh-century king, was excavated at Sutton Hoo, near Woodbridge in Suffolk. The tomb contained an astonishing collection of treasures, weapons of war and domestic utensils, objects of value and of religious significance. See James Campbell (ed.), *The Anglo-Saxons* (London: Phaidon Press, 1982), pp. 32–3.

7 *Beowulf*, ed. Porter, l. 27.

8 Ibid., l. 2820.

9 Ibid., ll. 3180–2.

10 Ibid., l. 72.

11 Ibid., ll. 76, 96.

12 *Guthlac* is translated in Bradley, *Anglo-Saxon Poetry*, pp. 248–83.

13 'The monsters are not an inexplicable blunder of taste; they are essential, fundamentally allied to the underlying ideas of the poem, which give it its lofty tone and high seriousness.' Tolkien in Nicholson (ed.), *An Anthology of 'Beowulf' Criticism*, p. 68. It was, Tolkien claims, at a 'fusion-point of imagination', not through an intellectual reconciliation, that the creatures of Germanic myth became synthesized with Christian doctrines.

14 *The Battle of Maldon*, ed. E. V. Gordon (London: Methuen, 1937), quotes the Old English original for this passage, p. 10.

15 A map of the assumed location of the battle is provided in Gordon (ed.), *The Battle of Maldon*, facing page 1. The phrase occurs at l. 66.

16 Ibid., ll. 312–13.

17 Ibid., l. 45.

18 Ibid., l. 86.

19 Ibid., l. 89.

20 See Katherine O'Brien O'Keeffe, 'Heroic Values and Christian Ethics', in Godden and Lapidge (eds.), *Cambridge Companion to Old English*, p. 119.

21 'While the Anglo-Saxons had been content with England, for the Vikings the known world was not big enough.' Lloyd and Jennifer Laing, *Anglo-Saxon England* (Routledge and Kegan Paul, 1979; London: Granada, 1982), p. 177.

22 Tacitus, *Germania*, trans. S. A. Handford (Harmondsworth: Penguin, 1948, revised 1970), p. 113.

CHAPTER 3. ELEGIAC POETRY

1 A text of *The Ruin* appears in Hamer (ed.), *A Choice of Anglo-Saxon Verse*, pp. 26–8.
2 See Hamer (ed.), *A Choice of Anglo-Saxon Verse*, p. 26.
3 Ibid.
4 Bede, *Ecclesiastical History*, pp. 129–30.
5 For the development of towns see Lloyd and Laing, *Anglo-Saxon England*, pp. 187–97; and Campbell, *The Anglo-Saxons*, pp. 152–3.
6 *The Wanderer*, ed. R. F. Leslie (Manchester: Manchester University Press, 1966).
7 William Wordsworth, 'Lines (Written a few miles above Tintern Abbey)', l. 29, in Michael Mason (ed.), *Lyrical Ballads* (London: Longman, 1992), p. 209.
8 *winsalo*, *The Wanderer*, ed. R. F. Leslie, l. 78.
9 *middangeard*, ibid., l. 75.
10 I have emphasized the co-existence of Christian and pagan elements by importing some words and phrases from the *King James Bible*, composed, of course, centuries after the Old English poem. See especially 1 Corinthians, 13: 4, reading 'wisdom' for 'charity'.
11 The song is marked off from the narrative by an introduction, *þas word acwið* ('I say this word'), and by a clear rhetorical and metrical structure that marks it off from the rest of the poem:

> *Hwaer cwom mearg? Hwaer cwom mago?*
> *Hwaer cwom maþ þumgyfa?*
> *Hwaer cwom symbla gesetu? Hwaer sindon seledreamas?*
> *Eala beorht bune! Eala byrnwiga!*
> *Eala þeodnes þrym!*

(Leslie, ll. 92–5)

12 Again the closing prayer is delineated from the rest of the monologue by a narrative marker: '*Swa cwaeð snottor on mode*' (Leslie, l. 111).
13 *The Seafarer*, ed. I. L. Gordon (London: Methuen, 1960).
14 See J. C. Pope (*Seven Old English Poems*), who actually divides the poem between '1st Seaf.' and '2nd Seaf.'.
15 '*Hungor*' literally means 'hunger'; but I agree with Gordon (*The Seafarer*, note on l. 11) that '*hungor* may imply more than the literal meaning here, and include figuratively the pangs of loneliness and suffering that gnaw at the Seafarer's heart'.
16 See Gordon (ed.), *The Battle of Maldon*, pp. 7–9.
17 *flaeschoma* ('covering of flesh, body'), *The Seafarer*, ed. I. L. Gordon, l. 94.

CHAPTER 4. CHRISTIAN POETRY

1 *The Dream of the Rood*, eds. Bruce Dickins and Alan Ross (London: Methuen, 1934, 4th edition 1954, revised 1960); and Michael Swanton, *The Dream of the Rood* (Manchester: Manchester University Press, 1970; revised edition, Exeter: University of Exeter Press, 1987).

2 See Dickins and Ross, pp. 1–13; Swanton, pp. 9–38.

3 See Dickins and Ross, pp. 13–16.

4 Hamer (ed.), *A Choice of Anglo-Saxon Verse*, p. 159. Earlier editors and critics thought the poem consisted of two halves, possibly by different hands, the second half certainly regarded as poetically inferior (see Dickins and Ross, p. 18). But compare Swanton, who declares the poem 'a coherent and unified whole' (p. 76).

5 For the ambivalence of *laene* see Christine Fell, 'Perceptions of Transience', in Godden and Lapidge (eds.), *The Cambridge Companion to Old English Literature*, p. 174.

6 One of the *Riddles*, the solution to which is 'beam' (a word that could, and here does, mean tree, ship, log, cup, or cross), conveys this tactile veneration of the Cross: 'Friends often pass me from hand to hand/And I am kissed by ladies and courteous men'. For a translation see *The Battle of Maldon and Other English Poems*, trans. Kevin Crossley-Holland, ed. Bruce Mitchell (London: Macmillan, 1965), p. 62. All three forms of relationship to the Cross are also featured in the *Dream*, where the Cross is 'widely worshipped' (l. 119); worn or traced as an insignia: 'no-one who bears/Bright in his breast this best of all signs' (ll. 155–6); and formulated in words: 'reveal your vision to the world in words' (l. 134). For translations of the relevant riddles, helpfully titled (so you don't have to guess the solution), as *Sword-Rack* and *Beam*, see Crossley-Holland and Mitchell, pp. 61–2.

7 See S. Allott, *Alcuin of York* (York, 1974), pp. 165–6.

8 Swanton (ed.) *The Dream of the Rood*, l. 39.

9 Crossley-Holland and Mitchell, *The Battle of Maldon*, p. 126.

10 Barbara C. Raw, 'Biblical Literature: The New Testament', in Godden and Lapidge (eds.), *The Cambridge Companion to Old English Literature*, pp. 238–9.

11 J. C. Pope, *Seven Old English Poems*, p. 44.

12 Swanton (ed.), *The Dream of the Rood*, 1. 41.

13 Ibid., ll. 72–3.

14 See Saint Ignatius of Loyola, *Personal Writings*, trans. Joseph A. Munitz and Philip Endean (Harmondsworth: Penguin, 1996).

15 John Milton, *Paradise Lost*, bk. i, ll. 105–8. *The Poems of John Milton*, ed.

Helen Darbishire (Oxford: Oxford University Press, 1961).

16 *Beowulf*, ed. Porter, ll. 530–610.

17 *The Battle of Maldon*, ed. E. V. Gordon, l. 11.

CHAPTER 5. LOVE POETRY

1 A text of *The Wife's Lament* can be found in Hamer (ed), *A Choice of Anglo-Saxon Verse*, pp. 72–4.

2 *Beowulf*, ed. Porter, ll. 612–30.

3 For text and translation of *The Husband's Message*, see Hamer (ed.), *A Choice of Anglo-Saxon Verse*, pp. 78–81. The extract translated here was published in the *Christian Poetry Review*, 6 (April 1997), p. 8.

4 A text of *Wulf and Eadwacer* can be found in Hamer (ed), *A Choice of Anglo-Saxon Verse*, p. 84.

Bibliography

EDITIONS

The Battle of Maldon, ed. E. V. Gordon (London: Methuen, 1937).

The Battle of Maldon, ed. D. G. Scragg (Manchester: Manchester University Press, 1981).

Beowulf and the Fight at Finnsburg, ed. Fr. Klaeber, (1992; 3rd edition, Boston: D. C. Heath, 1950).

Beowulf, ed. C. L. Wrenn, revised W. F. Bolton (first published London: Harrap, 1973; fifth edition Exeter: Exeter University Press, 1996).

Beowulf, ed. John Porter (Frithgarth: Anglo-Saxon Books, 1991).

Beowulf: A Student's Edition, ed. George Jack (Oxford: Clarendon, 1994).

Doane, A. N., ed., *Anglo-Saxon Manuscripts in Microfiche Facsimile* (Binghamton, NY: Centre for Mediaeval and Renaissance Studies, vols. 1–2: 1994, vol. 3: 1995, vol. 4: 1996).

The Dream of the Rood, ed. Michael Swanton (Manchester: Manchester University Press, 1970; revised edition, Exeter: University of Exeter Press, 1987).

The Dream of the Rood, eds. Bruce Dickins and Alan Ross (London: Methuen, 1934, 4th edition 1954, revised 1960).

The Seafarer, ed. I. L. Gordon (London: Methuen, 1960).

Genesis A: A New Edition, ed. A. N. Doane (Madison, Wis.: University of Wisconsin Press, 1978).

Sweet's Anglo-Saxon Reader, revised by C. T. Onions, (14th edition; Oxford: Clarendon Press, 1876, revised 1959).

The Wanderer, ed. R. F. Leslie (Manchester: Manchester University Press, 1966).

TRANSLATIONS

Alexander, Michael, *The Earliest English Poems* (Harmondsworth: Penguin, 1966).

106

Alexander, Michael (trans.), *Beowulf* (Harmondsworth: Penguin, 1973).

Bradley, S. A. J. (trans.), *Anglo-Saxon Poetry* (London: Dent, 1982).

Crossley-Holland, Kevin (trans.), and Bruce Mitchell (ed.), *The Battle of Maldon and Other English Poems* (London: Macmillan, 1965).

Gordon, R. K., *Anglo-Saxon Poetry* (London: Dent, 1926, revised 1954).

Hamer, Richard (ed.), *A Choice of Anglo-Saxon Verse* (London: Faber and Faber, 1979).

Heaney, Seamus, *Beowulf* (London: Faber and Faber, 1999).

Kennedy, Charles W., *Early English Christian Poetry* (London: Hollis and Carter, 1952).

HISTORY, CRITICISM, SCHOLARSHIP

Allott, S., *Alcuin of York* (York: William Sessions, 1974).

Aersten, H., and R. Bremmer (eds.), *The Cambridge Companion to Old English Poetry* (Amsterdam: VU University Press, 1994).

Bede, *Ecclesiastical History of the English People,* trans. Leo Sherley-Price, revised R. E. Latham (Harmondsworth: Penguin, 1955, revised 1990).

Blackburn, F. P., 'The Christian Coloring of the *Beowulf*', *PMLA* 12/2 (1897), 205–25.

Blair, P. Hunter, *An Introduction to Anglo-Saxon England* (Cambridge: Cambridge University Press, 2nd edition, 1977).

Caie, G. D., *The Judgement Day Theme in Old English Poetry* (Copenhagen: Nova, 1976).

Calder, D. G., et al., *Sources and Analogues to Old English Poetry* (Cambridge: D. S. Brewer, 1983).

Campbell, James (ed.), *The Anglo-Saxons* (London: Phaidon Press, 1982).

Crawford, S. J. (ed.), *The Old English Version of the Heptateuch, Aelfric's Treatise on the Old and New Testament and his Preface to Genesis* (Early English Text Society, 160; London: Humphrey Milford, Oxford University Press, 1922).

Damico, H. and A. H. Olsen (eds.), *New Readings on Woman in Old English Literature* (Bloomington, Ind.: Indiana University Press, 1990).

Fell, Christine, 'Perceptions of Transience', in *The Cambridge Companion to Old English Literature,* eds. Malcolm Godden and Michael Lapidge (Cambridge: Cambridge University Press, 1991), 172–89.

—— *Woman in Anglo-Saxon England* (London: British Museum Publications, 1984).

Frantzen, Allen J., *Desire for Origins: New Language, Old English, and Teaching the Tradition* (New Brunswick, NJ, and London: Rutgers University Press, 1990).

Gneuss, Helmut, 'The Old English Language', in *The Cambridge Companion to Old English Literature,* eds. Malcolm Godden and

Michael Lapidge (Cambridge: Cambridge University Press, 1991), 23–54.

Greenfield, S. B., and D. G. Calder, *A New Critical History of Old English Literature* (New York and London: New York University Press, 1986).

Hill, David, *An Atlas of Anglo-Saxon England 700–1066* (Oxford: Blackwell, 1981).

Holy Bible, New Revised Standard Edition (Cambridge: Cambridge University Press, 1989).

Howe, N., *Migration and Myth-making in Anglo-Saxon England* (New Haven: Yale University Press, 1989).

Laing, Lloyd and Jennifer, *Anglo-Saxon England* (Routledge and Kegan Paul, 1979; London: Granada, 1982).

Magoun, Francis P., Jr., 'The Oral-Formulaic Character of Anglo-Saxon Narrative Poetry', *Speculum*, 28 (1953), 446–67.

The New English Hymnal (Norwich: Canterbury Press, 1986).

Mitchell, Bruce, *An Invitation to Old English and Anglo-Saxon England* (Oxford: Blackwell, 1995).

Nicholson, Lewis E. (ed.), *An Anthology of 'Beowulf' Criticism* (Notre Dame, Ind.: Notre Dame University Press, 1963).

Niles, John D., 'Pagan Survivals and Popular Belief', in *The Cambridge Companion to Old English Literature*, eds. Malcolm Godden and Michael Lapidge (Cambridge: Cambridge University Press, 1991), 126–41.

North, R., *Heathen Gods in Old English Literature* (Cambridge: Cambridge University Press, 1997).

O'Keeffe, Katherine O'Brien, 'Heroic Values and Christian Ethics', in *The Cambridge Companion to Old English Literature*, eds. Malcolm Godden and Michael Lapidge (Cambridge: Cambridge University Press, 1991), 107–25.

Pollington, Stephen, *An Introduction to the Old English Language and its Literature* (Frithgarth: Anglo-Saxon Books, 1994, revised 1996).

Pope, J. C., *Seven Old English Poems* (New York: Bobbs-Merrill, 1966; revised edition, New York: Norton, 1981).

Raw, Barbara C., *The Art and Background of Old English Poetry* (London: Edward Arnold, 1978).

—— 'Biblical Literature: the New Testament', in *The Cambridge Companion to Old English Literature*, eds. Malcolm Godden and Michael Lapidge (Cambridge: Cambridge University Press, 1991), 227–42.

Robinson, F. C., 'Beowulf', in *The Cambridge Companion to Old English Literature*, eds. Malcolm Godden and Michael Lapidge (Cambridge: Cambridge University Press, 1991), 142–59.

—— *Beowulf and the Appositive Style* (Knoxville, Tenn.: University of Tennessee Press, 1985).

St Ignatius of Loyola, *Personal Writings*, trans. Joseph A. Munitz and Philip Endean (Harmondsworth: Penguin, 1996).

Scragg, D. (ed.), *The Battle of Maldon A.D. 991* (Oxford: Blackwell, 1991).

Shippey, T. A., *Old English Verse* (London: Hutchinson, 1972).

—— *Poems of Wisdom and Learning in Old English* (Cambridge: Cambridge University Press, 1976).

Swanton, M., 'The *Wife's Lament* and *The Husband's Message*: A Reconsideration', *Anglia*, 82 (1964), 269–90.

Tacitus, *Germania*, trans. S. A. Handford (Harmondsworth: Penguin, 1948, revised 1970).

Tolkien, J. R. R., 'Beowulf: The Monsters and the Critics', *Proceedings of the British Academy*, 22 (1936); reprinted in Lewis E. Nicholson (ed.), *An Anthology of 'Beowulf' Criticism* (Notre Dame, Ind.: Notre Dame University Press, 1963), pp. 51–104.

Whitelock, Dorothy, *The Audience of Beowulf* (Oxford: Clarendon, 1951).

Index

110

WRITERS AND THEIR WORK

RECENT & FORTHCOMING TITLES

Title	Author
Peter Ackroyd	*Susana Onega*
Kingsley Amis	*Richard Bradford*
Anglo-Saxon Verse	*Graham Holderness*
Antony and Cleopatra	*Ken Parker*
As You Like It	*Penny Gay*
W.H. Auden	*Stan Smith*
Alan Ayckbourn	*Michael Holt*
J.G. Ballard	*Michel Delville*
Aphra Behn	*Sue Wiseman*
John Betjeman	*Dennis Brown*
Edward Bond	*Michael Mangan*
Anne Brontë	*Betty Jay*
Emily Brontë	*Stevie Davies*
A.S. Byatt	*Richard Todd*
Caroline Drama	*Julie Sanders*
Angela Carter	*Lorna Sage*
Geoffrey Chaucer	*Steve Ellis*
Children's Literature	*Kimberley Reynolds*
Caryl Churchill	*Elaine Aston*
John Clare	*John Lucas*
S.T. Coleridge	*Stephen Bygrave*
Joseph Conrad	*Cedric Watts*
Crime Fiction	*Martin Priestman*
John Donne	*Stevie Davies*
Carol Ann Duffy	*Deryn Rees Jones*
George Eliot	*Josephine McDonagh*
English Translators of Homer	*Simeon Underwood*
Henry Fielding	*Jenny Uglow*
E.M. Forster	*Nicholas Royle*
Elizabeth Gaskell	*Kate Flint*
The *Gawain* Poet	*John Burrow*
The Georgian Poets	*Rennie Parker*
William Golding	*Kevin McCarron*
Graham Greene	*Peter Mudford*
Hamlet	*Ann Thompson & Neil Taylor*
Thomas Hardy	*Peter Widdowson*
David Hare	*Jeremy Ridgman*
Tony Harrison	*Joe Kelleher*
William Hazlitt	*J. B. Priestley; R. L. Brett (intro. by Michael Foot)*
Seamus Heaney	*Andrew Murphy*
George Herbert	*T.S. Eliot (intro. by Peter Porter)*
Henrik Ibsen	*Sally Ledger*
Henry James – The Later Writing	*Barbara Hardy*
James Joyce	*Steven Connor*
Julius Caesar	*Mary Hamer*
Franz Kafka	*Michael Wood*
William Langland: *Piers Plowman*	*Claire Marshall*
King Lear	*Terence Hawkes*
Philip Larkin	*Laurence Lerner*
D.H. Lawrence	*Linda Ruth Williams*
Doris Lessing	*Elizabeth Maslen*
C.S. Lewis	*William Gray*
David Lodge	*Bernard Bergonzi*
Christopher Marlowe	*Thomas Healy*
Andrew Marvell	*Annabel Patterson*
Ian McEwan	*Kiernan Ryan*
Measure for Measure	*Kate Chedgzoy*

RECENT & FORTHCOMING TITLES

Title	Author
A Midsummer Night's Dream	*Helen Hackett*
Vladimir Nabokov	*Neil Cornwell*
V. S. Naipaul	*Suman Gupta*
Walter Pater	*Laurel Brake*
Brian Patten	*Linda Cookson*
Harold Pinter	*Mark Batty*
Sylvia Plath	*Elisabeth Bronfen*
Jean Rhys	*Helen Carr*
Richard II	*Margaret Healy*
Dorothy Richardson	*Carol Watts*
John Wilmot, Earl of Rochester	*Germaine Greer*
Romeo and Juliet	*Sasha Roberts*
Christina Rossetti	*Kathryn Burlinson*
Salman Rushdie	*Damian Grant*
Paul Scott	*Jacqueline Banerjee*
The Sensation Novel	*Lyn Pykett*
P.B. Shelley	*Paul Hamilton*
Wole Soyinka	*Mpalive Msiska*
Edmund Spenser	*Colin Burrow*
J.R.R. Tolkien	*Charles Moseley*
Leo Tolstoy	*John Bayley*
Charles Tomlinson	*Tim Clark*
Anthony Trollope	*Andrew Sanders*
Victorian Quest Romance	*Robert Fraser*
Angus Wilson	*Peter Conradi*
Mary Wollstonecraft	*Jane Moore*
Women's Gothic	*Emma Clery*
Virginia Woolf	*Laura Marcus*
Working Class Fiction	*Ian Haywood*
W.B. Yeats	*Edward Larrissy*
Charlotte Yonge	*Alethea Hayter*